The Tidmarsh Family Tree

A story of twelve generations

Andrew Tidmarsh

Grosvenor House
Publishing Limited

All rights reserved
Copyright © Andrew Tidmarsh, 2024

The right of Andrew Tidmarsh to be identified as the author of this
work has been asserted in accordance with Section 78
of the Copyright, Designs and Patents Act 1988

The book cover is copyright to Andrew Tidmarsh

This book is published by
Grosvenor House Publishing Ltd
Link House
140 The Broadway, Tolworth, Surrey, KT6 7HT.
www.grosvenorhousepublishing.co.uk

This book is sold subject to the conditions that it shall not, by way of
trade or otherwise, be lent, resold, hired out or otherwise circulated
without the author's or publisher's prior consent in any form of
binding or cover other than that in which it is published and
without a similar condition including this condition being
imposed on the subsequent purchaser.

A CIP record for this book
is available from the British Library

ISBN 978-1-80381-761-3

Dedicated to my father, Reginald Tidmarsh, the last of the children of George and Daisy, my Aunty Audrey, who started the whole thing off and the memory of my grandfather, the man who I will always aspire to be.

Contents

Preface		vii
Acknowledgements		ix
Introduction		1
History of the Tidmarsh name		17
West Oxfordshire	family levels 1 and 2	22
Gloucestershire	family levels 3, 4, 5 and 6 (part)	26
West Oxfordshire—The Return	family levels 6 (part), 7, 8 and 9	32
Oxfordshire to East London	family levels 10 (part), 11 and 12	45
London	Family levels 11 and 12	55
George Harry Tidmarsh	My Grandfather	56
Daisy Woodward	My Grandmother	58
The Great War	Four years when the world changed	64
	The King's Royal Rifle Corps	64
	Western Front	65
	Le Tréport	72
	Aftermath	74
	Salvation Army	76
	George's Army Documents	80
	Epilogue	86

The Hospitals	Lewisham and The Miller	88
Family and Reflections	A few memories	92
The Family Trees	Twelve generations	104
	Tree data	105
	Levels 1—5	109
	Levels 6-12	110
	Reuben and Elizabeth	111
	Woodward family	112
Conclusion		113
Appendix 1	A letter from Audrey	114
Appendix 2	A letter from Stonesfield	115
Appendix 3	A letter from Reg	116
Afterword		117

Preface

Many kind permissions and a certain number of liberties have been taken in the preparation of this story; I will try to mention them all in one way or another but my particular thanks go to the people that take an interest in genealogy and local history and are only too keen to help out where they can.

My search started as a result of a family tree started by my Aunty Audrey, so a lot of groundwork had already been done and I took out a subscription to genealogy website Ancestry.co.uk which proved invaluable in tracking down characters and documents.

The search through twelve generations of my family tree at times became a little confusing, so I started to write a narrative to add some context to what is really just a large collection of boxes, inter-connected with a lot of lines. As I became more involved in the story the narrative took on a life of its own and I have tried to make it as interesting as possible. The connection made with the names in the boxes is personal to the reader, but there are a few small stories, adventures, mishaps and disasters in there as all of our ancestors had lives that reflected the events going on around them at the time. But it was always just going to be a brief historical background narrative, until I got to my grandparents.

George Tidmarsh, a quiet, clever, fairly unassuming man who had a profound effect on his children, my cousins and me. Daisy Woodward, a larger than life, pocket-sized dynamo of a woman who was a perfect balance to George's measured calmness. Given the life experiences of my grandfather, I thought I would gather some memories and anecdotes from my parents and cousins and write a separate narrative. My cousins, as always, were a constant source of information and amusement, all of us consistent in wanting to retain the memory of this man. In this story I have looked at George as a product of those that came before him, so it made sense to combine the family history and his story together in one narrative.

This is that narrative.

Acknowledgements

With thanks to:

My brothers and cousins from the UK, Australia and the US

Karen Tidmarsh

Lindsey Sellar, churchwarden of St. James the Great parish church, Stonesfield, to whom I will be forever grateful

Jo Paton, the parish administrator and Leah, the archivist of St Mary's and All Saints, Charlbury

Anne Lovett and the wonderful volunteers of Charlbury Museum

Ken and Audrey Tidmarsh

Reg and Doreen Tidmarsh

Findmygrave.co.uk

Deceasedonline.com

Ancestry.co.uk

Salvation Army International Heritage Centre

Kings Royal Rifles Association

Forces War Records

Lewisham Heritage

National Archives

Wartime Memories Project

Wikipedia

Passchendaele 1917: the Third Battle of Ypres in photographs—Chris McNab

The Times publications: First World War—Peter Chasseaud

Lost Hospitals of London

www.houseofnames.com

Neil Melrose and Michael Green of Stonesfield village

Introduction

I have always been fascinated by the stories told about my grandfather, from his wartime exploits, the events that clouded his opinions about his family, the story of 'Aunt Doll' (more of her later) and his life as a hospital porter. I never really gave much thought to the generations that came before him though, until recently.

My Aunty Audrey started to compile a family tree many years ago and made a significant journey into the Tidmarsh family history, going back to James and Mary Tidmarsh in the eighteenth century. Earlier this year I decided to see if I could enhance the tree to bring it up to date and maybe add a few generations. This seemingly straightforward task was not in any way straightforward; however, it was fascinating and became almost an obsession. It took me on a journey of nearly 500 years into English history and gave me an insight into generations of family that lived in both the countryside and the city, followed the birth of the modern industrialised age as well as one civil and two world wars. They survived hardships, poverty, sickness, death and the horrors of trench warfare. This is not an extensive history, but, at the time of writing, follows the family back to the 1500s, using the tree first researched and recorded by my auntie, along with personal visits to the places where our forefathers were born, baptised, married and buried and endless hours combing through civil and military ancestry websites, parish archives and graveyards. It's a story that starts in the picturesque villages of the Cotswolds in Oxfordshire and travels to the brutal streets and dockyards around Silvertown and West Ham.

Because of my grandfather's experiences in WWI, I have also included some separate chapters, one for his regiment, one for the horrors he would have experienced on the Western Front and one for the Salvation Army field services, all of which are an integral part of this story and hopefully add some historical context to that period.

My family history document has been created in three parts, all of which are contained here:

1. A tree plan tracing the family line from 1570, which in itself is broken into three sections for ease of reading.
2. A data file spreadsheet, designed to be the information portal for the tree plan.
3. This narrative, containing some background information to add context to the tree plan.

The tree is also plotted on Ancestry.co.uk under the title **Tidmarsh Family Tree.**

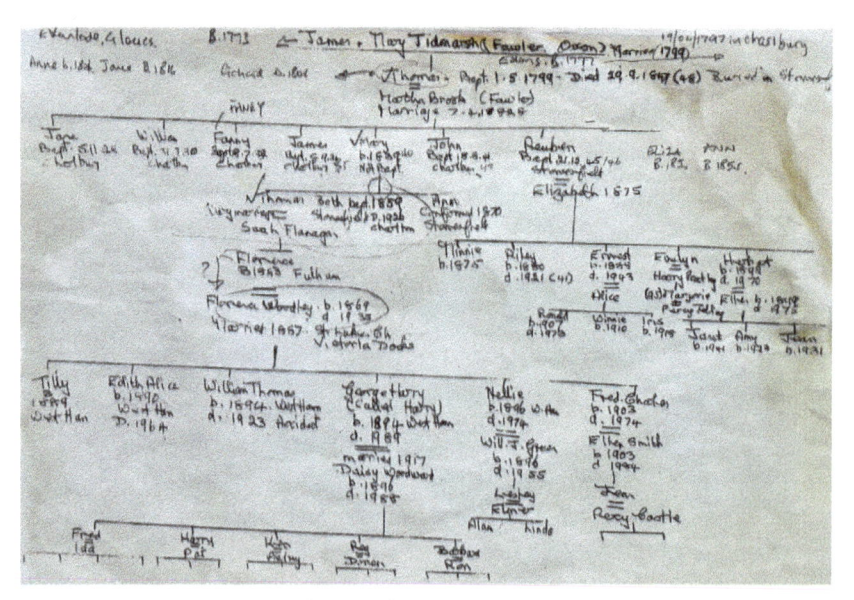

This was the starting point.

My family tree has been created in 'levels', starting at level 1 with John and Ann Tidmarsh from the Broadwell area of West Oxfordshire. Over the next nine generations, the Tidmarshes move around Gloucestershire and Oxfordshire before one of our ancestors made the move south to London.

The levels descend through the family line for twelve generations, to the children of my grandparents George and Daisy. Later on in the narrative I have used the denotations of Snr and Jnr as sometimes there are a lot of similar names. In Oxfordshire, it was traditional for most Tidmarsh families to call the first son Thomas. In eleven generations of my family line there are three Johns, two Richards, three Thomases, one James, one Mary and one George. So, we kind of bucked the trend a bit, especially with one female in the line I suspect.

The searches initially focussed on five main parishes—Broadwell, Stonesfield and Charlbury in Oxfordshire and Adlestrop and Evenlode in Gloucestershire—which takes the story from the mid-1500s to the mid-1800s before the family line migrated to London.

Both Karen and I will forever be grateful to the churchwarden of St James parish Church in Stonesfield, Lindsey Sellar. Hers was the first church we visited and her willingness to open up the parish archives to total strangers was an act of kindness that not only helped us out with our search but ignited a determination to find out as much as I could about how this family got to where we are today.

I'm also thankful to Jo Paton, the parish administrator of Charlbury who allowed us access to their records and set up a meeting with the village archivist.

I have also plotted the family tree of my Gt x 4 Uncle Rueben and Aunt Elizabeth as it was included in my auntie's family tree and also because theirs was the first family gravestone I found when researching, which was a great thrill.

Also included are the descendants of Sarah Flanagan, who bore two children with my great grandfather, Thomas, prior to his marriage to my great grandmother and the children of Mary Tidmarsh, my gt x 2 grandmother, as a result of her marriage to Frederick Stayte.

Quite often there are many variations of our name in historical documents—Tidmarsh, Titmarsh, Tydmarsh for instance, even Pedmarsh in one document. Merrell Tidmarsh is described in different documents as Meriel and Merit. When Martha Tidmarsh remarried William, their surname is described as Pantin and Paintin in different documents (I stuck with the former). I found some Pantin gravestones in Charlbury churchyard, no direct relations that I can ascertain, but no doubt relations of William, which adds a little interest and intrigue.

Just to further confuse things, in 1582 Britain changed from the Julian calendar to the Gregorian calendar, so New Year's Day moved from 25 March to 1 January and eleven days were dropped from September of that year. This just adds to the fun of trying to find people in history that seem to disappear without trace and then reappear when you least expect it. The other issue I experienced was the condition of the gravestones. Those made from softer types of stone weather easily and don't stand the test of time and a lot of churches lose track of graveyard maps before the eighteenth century, which makes finding resting places quite difficult, if in fact a headstone was there in the first place. Sarah Flanagan, probably not legally a Tidmarsh yet a key part in this family history, as we shall see later, was buried in a paupers' or 'common' grave with at least ten other people in the same plot, the exact location of which has been lost in time. One can only use what information the graveyard administrators have to find an approximate area but, for me, just knowing that they are there can be enough, especially in the sad case of Sarah and her daughter Lily Maud.

The family story is a dramatic contrast of opposites, from the rolling open countryside of the Cotswolds, to the brutal industrial harshness of east London's docklands and then the post-war council estates of south-east London.

There are two instances when we may not have existed—if Mary had not had illegitimate children or they had taken the surname of the man she later married and if Sarah Flanagan had not died. In the first instance, we would probably have the surname of Stayte. In the second instance, there would be a Tidmarsh family line—but it wouldn't be us.

There are several mysteries that I will try and cover as best I can:

- Who was Cecilia Parkin and what happened to her?
- What happened to Thomas from the age of around ten in Oxfordshire to when he appears as a teenager in east London?
- What was the German connection with the Woodward family and did they flee to England?
- What was the Jewish connection with the Woodwards?
- What was the cause of Doll's mental illness?

There is also my grandfathers' story of bravery in the mud and chaos of Passchendaele during WWI, which I have attempted to add historical context to later on.

As well as trying to track down the ancestors of John and Ann Tidmarsh, pre-sixteenth century, I have also started researching the family tree of Daisy Woodward's family and that of my own mother's family, the Howards and the Haymes—I did say it had become an obsession. All of these family trees are on Ancestry.co.uk which enables contributors to share information when trees inter-relate. I recently made contact with a descendent of Sarah Flanagan's great grandson, descending from Sarah's surviving daughter, Florence, who told me where Florence and her husband Walter Day were buried, so there's a lot of people out there pursuing an interest in their family's history, myself included, who will come across family that they are related to direcly or indirectly.

In 1538, a new law required every Church of England parish priest to record baptisms, marriages and burials, a parish being a small administrative district with its own church, priest (size of parish permitting) and possibly a clerk. This is good news when searching for ancestors, but the information is only as good as the attention to detail of the clerk or scribe. Some records are meticulous and in beautiful writing, others not so much as some clerks had a habit of rushing everything at the last minute. One hopes that John, my gt x 10 grandfather, a clerk of Broadwell, was one of the former.

Another key development in the search for ancestors came with the Rose Act of 1813 which decreed that all baptisms, marriages and burials were recorded in a consistent manner, displaying a set list of information where we can establish dates, parental details, ages and occupations.

So, from the very basic information, if indeed any information existed, that can be gleaned in the sixteenth century as we approach the nineteenth century, the search for family becomes more structured and most of the time easier.

With regard to scandal, which everyone secretly hopes to uncover, we have a few instances:

Illegitimate children were a shameful secret, even in the early Victorian years, though as her reign reached its height, prudish attitudes reached their peak. Not to be outdone, Mary Tidmarsh had two. We know that they kept the Tidmarsh name, which is a good thing for the family as I know it. What isn't so well advertised is that four years prior to the birth of Mary's first child, Anne, her sister Jane gave birth to a daughter, Eliza, who was looked after by her grandparents Richard and Martha.

There's the strange case of Edith Alice, daughter of Thomas Tidmarsh and Francis Woodley. Deemed incapable of looking after herself, she manages to avoid the usual description in early censuses of mentally challenged children, but there is no description that I can find about what was wrong with her. In conversation with members of the family, there is a suggestion that she had contracted syphilis from her mother, contracted from her husband, whilst she was pregnant with Edith. Mental disorders can arise as a result of this condition so it may be the case, who knows.

Sarah Flanagan, the young woman of Irish decent that my great grandfather had two children with, is one of the more enigmatic characters in this story. There is no evidence that Thomas and Sarah were married and Thomas married Florence Woodley within a year of Sarah's death. So, possibly another two illegitimate children and a line of the Tidmarsh family that we may never know. Apart from Grandad's experiences in WWI, the story of Sarah was the saddest for me.

Cecilia Parkin, the strange case of an eighteen-month-old girl, born in Battersea but recorded as part of the household of Thomas and Florence's family in West Ham in 1911. No one alive remembers her; she disappears from the household before the next census in 1921, into a fog of mystery. If Thomas didn't want anyone to know about her, it would have been easy to leave her off. Thomas was often less than accurate in recording certain pieces of information and adoption as we know it didn't start until 1927, so records before that are very sparse. I am currently searching through the Dr Barnardo's organisation and Adopted.com but it's likely this will remain a mystery.

The family graves I have uncovered so far have not been in good condition and a lot of them are barely readable, but sometimes old graves contain more information about the person than written records and it also gives one a chance to sign up to the wonderfully named website—www.deceasedonline.com.

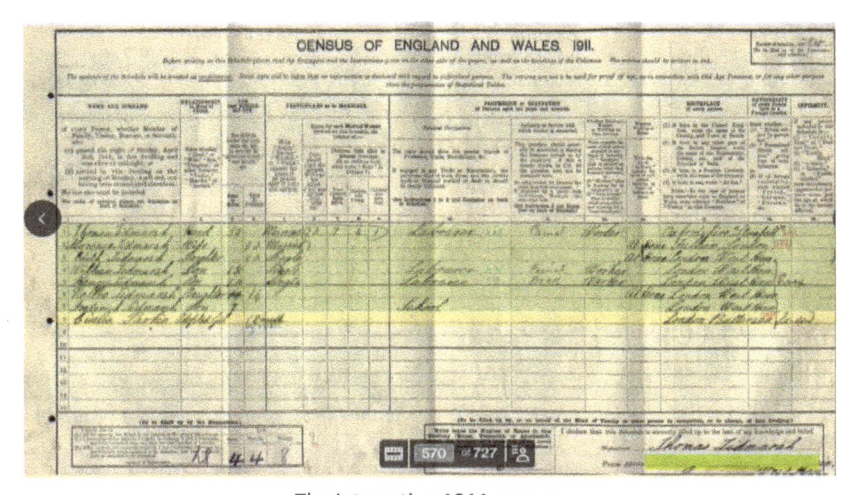

The interesting 1911 census.

Graveyard hunting—my new favourite hobby.

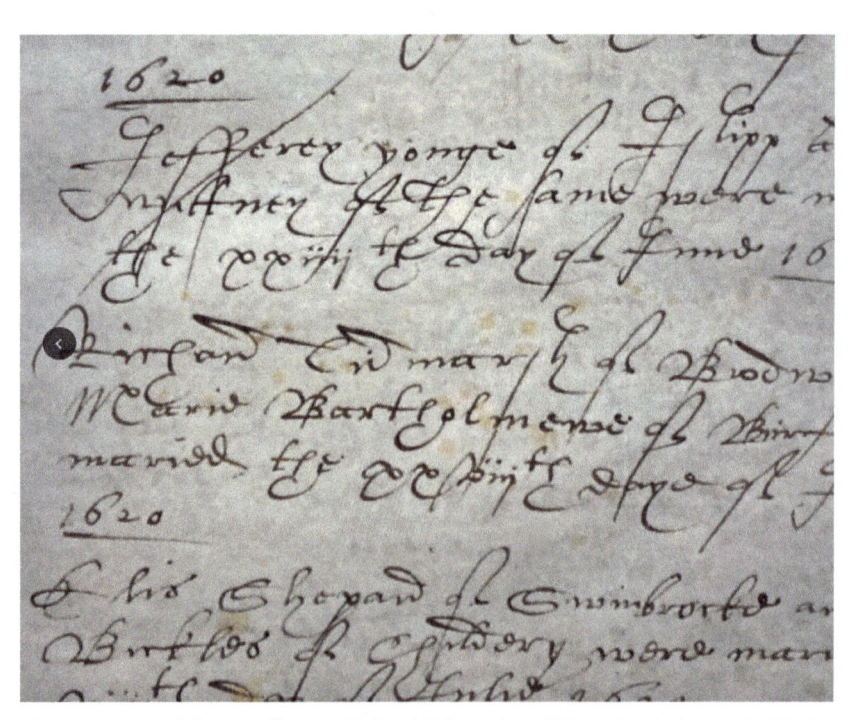

Contrasting wedding certificates, Richard Tidmarsh and Mary Bartholomew in 1620, the barest of information but beautiful handwriting, ink on parchment.

The wedding certificate of George Tidmarsh and Daisy Woodward.
The same lovely writing but, in accordance with the Rose Act,
using a pre-printed form with a plethora of useful information.
This document was later changed to reflect George's official name.

Modern websites are a powerful way of processing information, but the further back in time one goes, the sparser the information and the more fanciful the spellings. Thanks to William the Conqueror (not a sentiment our Anglo-Saxon forefathers would adhere to I suspect) and his Domesday project of 1086, this country makes a habit of recording its citizens and the ten-yearly census, commencing 1901 (except for 1941, which was cancelled due to the war) is an invaluable source of information—household, number of rooms, inhabitants, occupations—all on one page. Births, deaths and baptisms are meticulously kept until before the fifteenth century when things tend to get a little less informative, mostly led by the local parish church, buildings that are monuments to British history and the lives of its people. Churches are invaluable sources of information and local interest, with graveyards full of memorials in different states of repair, from the solid granite cross of Reuben and Elizabeth to the barely readable sandstone of Samuel (ii) (son of Richard and Merrell) to the elegance of my great grandparents and great uncle, with its floral designs and lead-lined inscription. Then to the common graves where ten to twelve people were laid in the same plot, overlooked by the rows of centuries-old gravestones, removed to make way for newer stones and left to prop up the graveyard or cemetery walls like rows of ancient guardians.

Here are some random samples of the documentation encountered along the way …

From the Stonesfield archives.

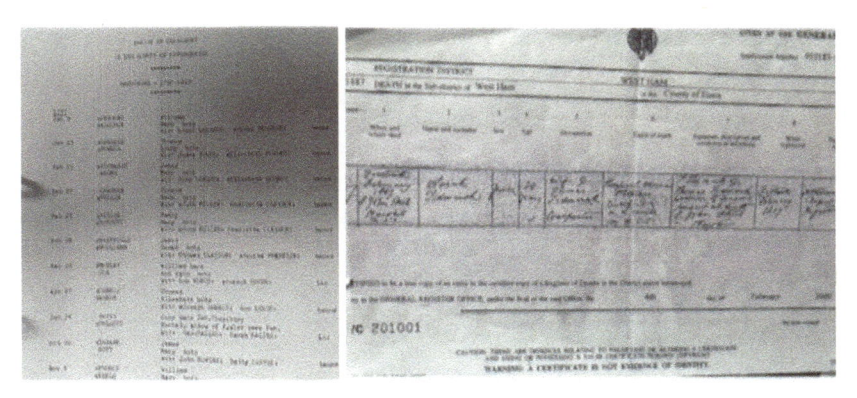

From the Charlbury archives. Birth, death & Marriage certificates.

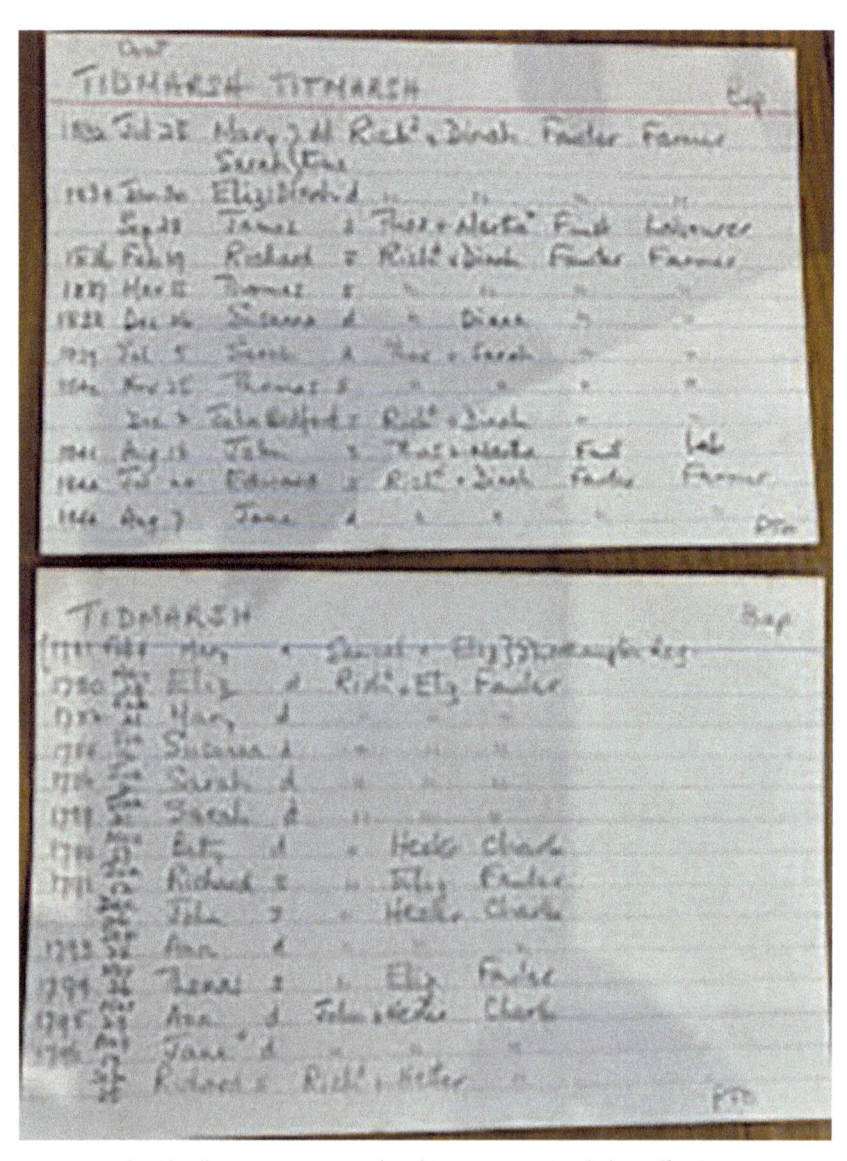

The Charlbury Museum card archive system, simple but effective.

THE TIDMARSH FAMILY TREE

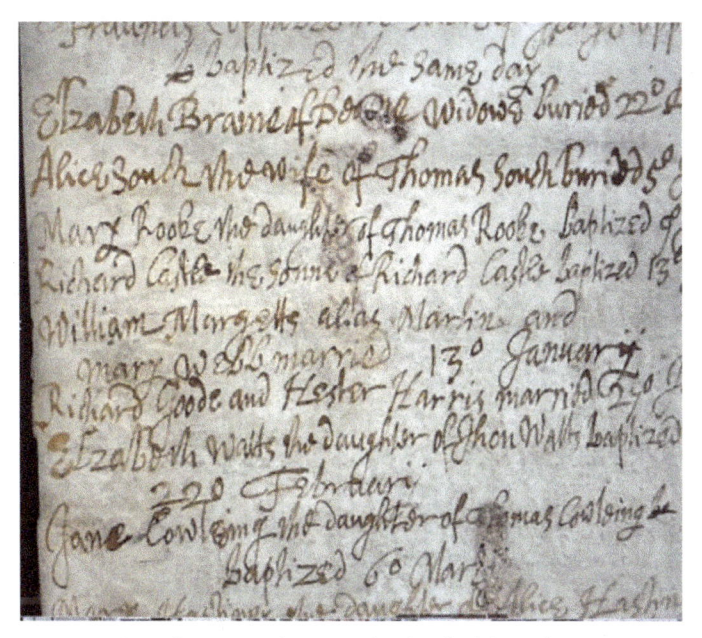

Baptism of Mary Rook, 1630—hard to find, but it's there!

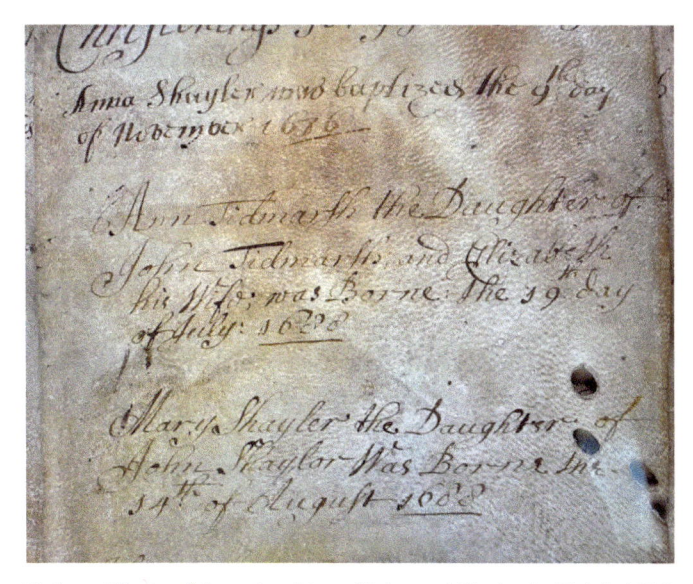

Birth certificate of Ann, daughter of John and Elizabeth, 19 July 1688,
written by quill on parchment, in old English script,
a beautiful example of seventeenth century parish clerical records.

13

CERTIFIED COPY OF AN ENTRY OF DEATH

GIVEN AT THE GENERAL REGISTER OFFICE

Application Number 13983686-7

REGISTRATION DISTRICT **Charlbury**

DEATH in the Sub-district of **Charlbury** **CHIPPING NORTON** in the County of **Oxford**

No.	When and where died	Name and surname	Sex	Age	Occupation	Cause of death	Signature, description and residence of informant	When registered	Signature of registrar
261	Twenty third February 1924 Tidmarsh Lane Charlbury R.D.	Mary Stayte	Female	85 years	Widow of Frederick Stayte Farm Labourer	(1) Old age (2) Heart failure certified by W.R.P. McKnight M.D.	L. Chapman daughter present at the death Tidmarsh Lane Charlbury	Twenty fifth February 1924	Jack Harvey Registrar

CERTIFIED to be a true copy of an entry in the certified copy of a Register of Deaths in the District above mentioned.
Given at the GENERAL REGISTER OFFICE, under the Seal of the said Office, the 10th day of July 2023

DYE 655753

CAUTION: THERE ARE OFFENCES RELATING TO FALSIFYING OR ALTERING A CERTIFICATE AND USING OR POSSESSING A FALSE CERTIFICATE ©CROWN COPYRIGHT
WARNING: A CERTIFICATE IS NOT EVIDENCE OF IDENTITY.

Death dertificate of Mary Tidmarsh (Stayte) who died of old age at eighty-five on 23 February 1924 in Charlbury. Her daughter Lettie Stayte (now Chapman) was present at her death. A doyen of the Tidmarsh family in my opinion.

```
           21  GILES    William    5 days
           28  WELLS    Elizabeth  10 wks
1852
Jan  18  TIDMARSH  Albyn       14
     19  GODDARD   Elizabeth   69
     29  HANKS     Elizabeth   15 wks
Apr   7  TIDMARSH  Ann         13 yrs   commonly named Ann DAVIS
     26  HOWES     Susan       65
May   8  MILLIN    Elizabeth   75
     24  BARRETT   Ann         70
Jun  24  MILLIN    Milpah      32
Jul   1  TIDMARSH  Henry       16 mos
Oct  28  TIDMARSH  Sarah       4 yrs
Nov  20  TOWNSEND  Edward      74
Dec   9  MAYCOCK   George      9 wks
     31  CLARE     Elizabeth   60
1853
Jan  10  MILLIN    Ann         2 yrs
     22  TIDMARSH  John        12 yrs
Feb  13  HUNT      Samuel      6 mos
     15  WING      Louisa      1 mo
     21  TUBB      Elizabeth   5 mos
Mar   2  COULING   Hannah      67
     13  PAXFORD   Mary        79
Apr  18  TIDMARSH  James       80
May   5  OSBORNE   Sarah       81   Fawler adjoining Stonesfield
     18  LOW       Hannah      79
Jul   2  LAUGHTON  James       78   sudden death Jun 27th
Aug  13  HOPKINS   Eliza Anne  1 mo
Oct  18  WARD      George      11 days
Dec  19  PAXFORD   William     81
1854
Jan  19  PAXFORD   Mary Anne   22
Mar  12  BUMPAS    Mary        70
     26  GARDNER   Peter       54
Apr  10  TUBB      Maria       36
May   4  TOWNSEND  Joseph      6 yrs
     30  BARRETT   John        77
     31  WING      Annetta     8 yrs 11 mos
Aug   1  OLIVER    Charles     45
     27  HICKMAN   Edmund      49   killed by accident Aug 24 - run
                                    waggon horses running aw
Sep   2  GRIFFIN   Henry       22
     16  GRIFFIN   Esther      36
Oct  13  MAYCOCK   Thomas      3 days
     29  MAYCOCK   Mary        31
Nov   7  DAVIS     Abel        41
     23  FIDLER    Georgiana   20
     28  GRIFFIN   Martha      59
```

Burial records of Tidmarsh clans, Stonesfield, Oxfordshire.

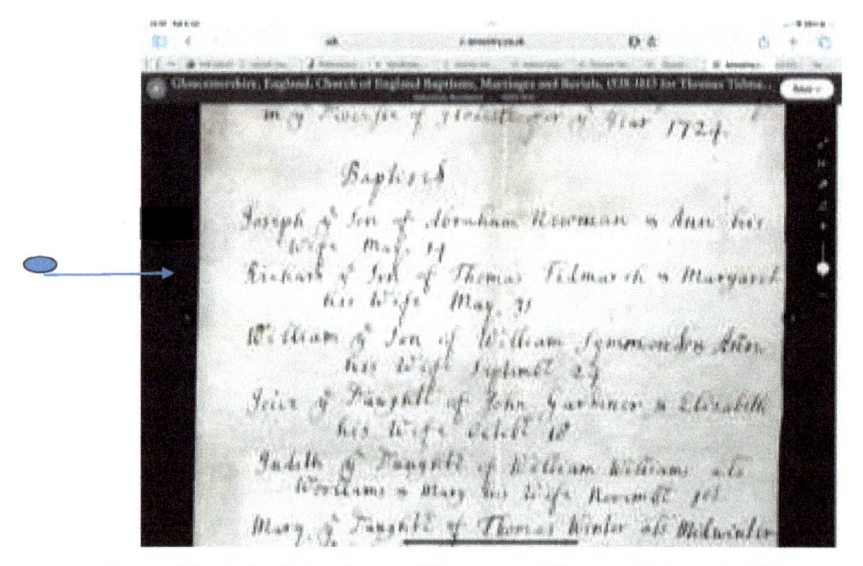

Baptism certificate for Richard, son of Thomas and Margaret Tidmarsh, 1724.

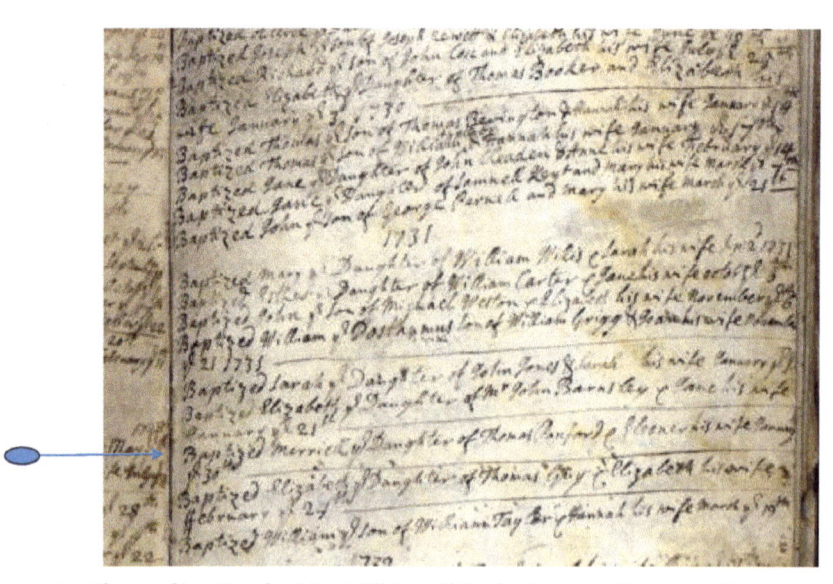

Certificate of baptism for Merriel (Merrell) Paxford, my gt x 5 grandmother.

History of the Tidmarsh Name

English: habitational name from Tidmarsh in Berkshire, which is named from Old English:

theod 'people' + *mersc* 'marsh'

Introduction

Whilst researching the history of the family, it proved evident that the further back you research, the harder the evidence is to come by. Parish and local government documentation becomes a lot less structured and quill and parchment takes over from paper and although some of the writing is beautiful, the wording is in old English and the ink can weep into parchment, making reading difficult. I have mentioned the entries of Tidmarsh habited villages in the Domesday Book, the 'great survey' which started recording life in England from 1086 as a result of a request by William the Conqueror, which was a foretaste of the modern censuses that supply so much useful information for government and genealogists alike. So, as the history of our families fades into the distance, companies like 'House of Names' can supply generic information based on their extensive historical research.

The results of this research can't focus on a particular branch of the family line, unless there were significant historical events to make that possible. Rather it is meant as a broad-brush point of reference.

Tidmarsh is a village in West Berkshire, mainly residential and agricultural, situated between the towns of Pangbourne and Theale in the vicinity of Reading.

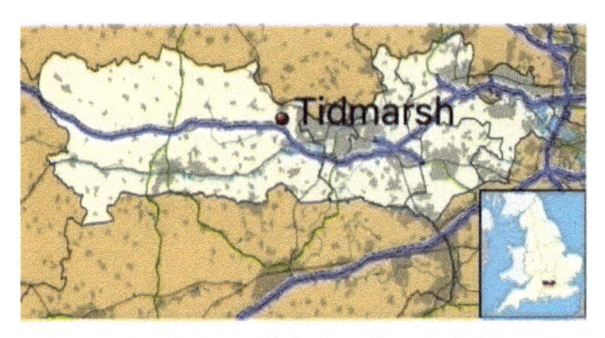

Location within Berkshire

Appearance of the Tidmarsh name

Their research has shown that our surname is of Anglo-Saxon origin, a culture that had a significant impact on English society, and as a result, we have followed and been part of the growth of the English nation. According to research carried out from the Domesday Book (1086), the Ragman Rolls (1291–1296), parish and local government documentation, the first recorded instance of the name 'Tidmarsh' or 'De Tidmarsh' was in Berkshire, within the parish of Tidmarsh. The parish Church of St. Laurence in Tidmarsh is a twelfth-century structure, part Norman, part early English style, like most churches of that time.

As I discovered in my family tree research, the Tidmarsh name has quite a few variations, this was confirmed when we visited Charlbury Museum and were given access to their records. The curator's note to us casually informed us not to worry too much about different spellings or locations as we were all probably related anyway! Some of the variations would be Tidemarsh, Titmarsh, De Todemarsh, Titmas, Titmus, Tidmarsh, Tidmas, Tidmass, Tidmuss, Tidmersh and Tidmershe. These spelling variations were frequent, even between father and son. It was common to find the same individual referred to with different spellings of their surname. The main reason for this is that scribes and parish clerks wrote down names according to their sound, rather than their spelling. The first

Tidmarsh parish church

'The church is partly Norman, and partly in the early English style; the doorway is a particularly fine specimen of Norman architecture: the ceiling of the chancel is of panelled oak, and there are two slabs of blue marble, with some ancient brasses.'
Lewis, Samuel, *A Topographical Dictionary of England*.
Institute of Historical Research, 1848.

record of the place name was Tedmerse in 1196 and it literally meant 'people's or common marsh'.

The family name was first referenced in the year 1315 when Stephen de Tydemersh of what is now Tidmarsh in Berkshire was recorded as holding estates in Kent.

The Saxons

The Saxons were a Teutonic tribe originally from northern Germany who began to settle in England in about the year 400 AD. Their first settlements were in Kent, on the south-east coast. Gradually, they probed north and westward from Kent and during the next four hundred years forced the ancient Britons back into Wales and Cornwall to the west. They won territories as far north as Lancashire and Yorkshire, pushing the Britons into Cumbria and Southern Scotland. The Angles, another Teutonic tribe, occupied the eastern coast, the south folk in Suffolk, the north folk in Norfolk. The Angles sometimes invaded as far north as Northumbria and the Scottish border. The Angle and Saxon cultures blended together as they came to dominate the country. For hundreds of years England was comprised of five independent Anglo-Saxon kingdoms until unification in the ninth century. By 1066, England, under Harold, was enjoying reasonable peace and prosperity. However, the Norman invasion and victory at the Battle of Hastings meant that the Anglo-Saxon landowners lost their property to the invaders. The Saxons were restive under Norman rule, and many moved northward to the Midlands, Lancashire and Yorkshire, where Norman influence was less pervasive.

As peace was restored, the Tidmarsh surname emerged as that of a notable English family in the county of Berkshire where they held a family seat. Later on, the name branched to Worcestershire, Wiltshire and Oxfordshire where they were also shown on tax records.

Migration

It's probably worth noting, for interest's sake more than anything, that many Tidmarsh's migrated to Ireland, America, Canada, Australia and New Zealand. My research bought up many records of such Tidmarsh migrants from the nineteenth and early twentieth centuries, journeys that were a lot more perilous than when my uncle Harry and his family departed for Australia in 1950. This could well explain the various sightings of Tidmarsh graves in the US by my cousins on their visits and records of businesses owned by Tidmarsh's in Australia.

Conclusion

From Saxon settlements, through the turmoil of the Norman invasion, the Tidmarsh (DeTidmarsh) family survive and are recorded as having a family seat in Berkshire, prior to their movement to what we now refer to as the Cotswolds. The families that settled in Oxfordshire are very likely to be the ancestors of the family I now know.

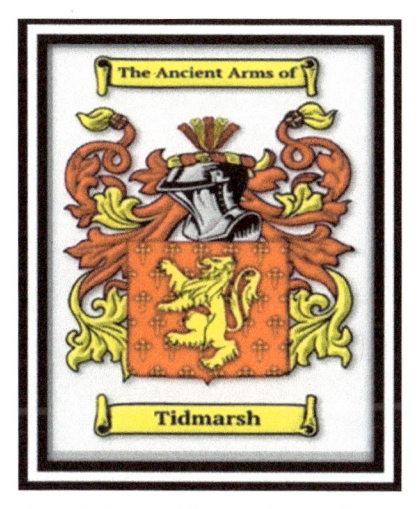

With acknowledgement to www.houseofnames.com.

Heraldry is a complex field, although the coat of arms is assured to be that of the Tidmarsh family. There is a suggestion that the Tidmarsh name can be traced back to the crusades, it may also be possible that it was never flown in battle, rather it adorned the walls of houses belonging to our more affluent ancestors in the Tidmarsh family homeland in Berkshire.

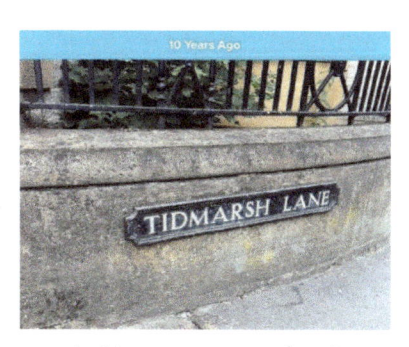

Just to prove we were here!

West Oxfordshire

Levels 1 and 2: 1570–1625

The reign of Elizabeth I, change from the Julian to Gregorian calendar

Broadwell

Location within Oxfordshire

Until the mid-1800s when **Thomas Tidmarsh** (my great grandfather) left Oxfordshire for the east end of London, the Tidmarsh men were predominantly yeomen and agricultural labourers and the women in service or later, gloveresses. This story commences in the small village of Broadwell in West Oxfordshire, close to the border with Gloucestershire. There were and probably still are an abundance of Tidmarsh clans scattered around Gloucestershire and West Oxfordshire and local church graveyards are full of Tidmarsh gravestones, many, unfortunately, too weather worn to read.

Broadwell is a quiet rural village, unmentioned in the Domesday Book, that grew up around the growth of agriculture in the area and the building of the three imposing manor houses that managed the surrounding estates. The population were predominantly yeomen, craftsmen, clerks, tradesmen and labourers working for or alongside and dependent on the larger landowners. When researching the family history and arriving at Broadwell as the birthplace of one of my distant ancestors, I was confused as to whether I was researching in Oxfordshire or Gloucestershire as local maps can be a little misleading, however, the village website proudly states 'Physically Oxfordshire, Postally Gloucestershire, Always Cotswolds'. For the sake of this story, I have used Oxfordshire, as more historical documents refer to it as so. Beside an imposing manor house situated on the outskirts of the village is the equally imposing (well, for me anyway) twelfth-century Church of St Peter and St Paul. Straddling the Monarch's Way[1] and set in a large quiet churchyard sheltered by huge ancient yew trees, this church would have carried out the usual services of funerals, weddings and baptisms. One baptism, carried out in 1570, was that of **John Tidmarsh,** my gt x 10 grandfather. Born in the same year into this rural farming community in Elizabethan times, it's likely his father was a smallholder (or yeoman) or agricultural labourer. He was employed as a clerk and he married a lady called **Ann**, also born in 1570 and whose maiden name is currently unknown. I'm not sure of the wedding date, but guests would have made most of the gifts or could contribute to the 'bridal ale', a rustic wedding feast. To be considered as legally binding, the marriage had to be consummated, which could involve the couple being accompanied to their marriage bed by the priest and other witnesses. I managed to find two children, Dinah and **Richard. John** died in 1636 at the age of sixty-six with his wife outliving him by just three years, when she died at sixty-nine years in 1639. Both are likely to be buried in Broadwell. Little is known of their daughter Dinah, but **Richard** my gt x 9 grandfather is now our main focus.

The year 1595 saw the first performance of *Romeo and Juliet* by 'The Lord Chamberlain's Men' in London, whilst the rural village of Broadwell saw the birth of **Richard Tidmarsh**. Like his father,

---

[1] *Monarch's Way marks the route taken by Charles II after his defeat at the Battle of Worcester in 1651.*

records are sparse, but the likelihood is that he followed in his father's footsteps as a clerk or followed his forefathers as a smallholder. His son went into agriculture after his death, so that could give us a clue.

Richard married **Mary Bartholomew.** As we now move into the seventeenth century, the poorer a girl was, the greater freedom she had in choosing a husband, but she was still expected to ask her parents for their blessing and money was not as much of a key factor. There were two children by this marriage that I can find thus far, Mary and **John,** my gt x 8 grandfather. I haven't been able to track their date of marriage as yet and there is sparse information about Mary, but **John** will now be the main focus. **Richard** died in 1663 at the age of sixty-eight. **Mary** died in 1634 at the age of thirty-five when her son **John** was only nine. It's my theory that **Richard** moved closer to Adlestrop in neighbouring Gloucestershire to be nearer to other branches of the Tidmarsh family after his bereavement, so this is where we go to next. But first, some images of the church at Broadwell.

St Peter and St Paul, Broadwell

Place of baptism for John and family.

A feature from the porch.

Looking up from the font.

Broadwell village, a grouping of Cotswold cottages around a small village green, a modern photo but I get the sense that this place has remained unchanged for centuries and is rather as my gt x 10 grandparents would have known it.

Gloucestershire

Levels 3, 4, 5 and 6 (part) 1625–1770

The reign of Charles I, Civil War and Commonwealth, Charles II, James II, William and Mary

Adlestrop

The Gloucestershire village of Adlestrop was a once bustling farming community, even boasting its own railway station until 1966. Its mention in the Domesday Book tells us that it was owned by the Abbey of Evesham in Warwickshire (demolished in the sixteenth century during the dissolution of the monasteries) and at the time, consisted of ten villagers, two smallholders, four slaves and one man-at-arms. Situated three miles east of Stow-on-the-Wold, on the border with Oxfordshire, it was the home to many branches of the Tidmarsh family, including ours, whose men were predominantly agricultural and general labourers and whose women were predominantly gloveresses. The village was the subject of a poem 'Adlestrop' by

Edward Thomas, a copy of which hangs in the church as a tribute to one of its patrons.[2]

St Mary Magdalene Church dates back to the thirteenth century and was rebuilt in the 1750s. **Thomas Tidmarsh** (1686–1782) was a church warden here.

St Mary Magdalene Parish Church.

Tidmarsh graves.

---

[2] *Edward Thomas (1878–1917) a British writer and poet, sometimes referred to as a war poet although few of his poems reflect his wartime experiences. 'Adlestrop' was written by chance in 1914. The reason I mention this, apart from the beauty of the poem, is that he was killed in 1917 at the battle of Arras where, as a 2nd Lieutenant in the Artists Rifle Corps he would have been fighting alongside other regiments of the British Expeditionary Force on the Western Front at the same time as my grandfather.*

Unfortunately, the church no longer keeps records this far back, nor does the Gloucestershire Archive, so plotting the location of family graves is virtually impossible.

So, it is here that the next part of the story starts with **John Tidmarsh**, my gt x 8 grandfather, an agricultural labourer, who was born in 1625. He married **Mary Rooke,** born in 1630 in Spelsbury, Oxfordshire, in the parish Church of St Edwards in Evenlode, on 16 April 1666, almost a month after the birth in March of their son **John**, my gt x 7 grandfather. I can only find evidence of one child as information about the family at this time is sparse and what documents can be found are written on parchment and often the ink has seeped through the parchment making them difficult to read. **Mary** died in the August of 1686. **John** died 12 years later in March of 1698; they were both buried in Adlestrop.

On 4 January 1666, **John and Mary's** son **John** (a popular Tidmarsh name) was born, whilst in the neighbouring village of Churchill, **Elizabeth Hiett** was born in 1664. The two were to marry in Adlestrop on 4 January 1685. If there was ever what I as an 'outsider' would call a quintessentially 'Cotswold' village, Churchill is it. They had four children—Ann, Elizabeth, John and in the November of 1686, **Thomas**, my gt x 6 grandfather.

Thomas, another generation of Adlestrop Tidmarshes who worked the land in these parts, was born in 1686 and married at twenty-four years old to a local girl, **Margaret Grimmett**, who was born in 1684. They were married on 18 May 1710 in the Church of St Leonard, Lower Lemington.

Thomas and Margaret had nine children—Ann, Elizabeth, John, Samuel, Thomas, Frances, James, Edmund and born in May 1724, **Richard**, my gt x 5 grandfather.

Richard married **Merrell Paxford** who was born in 1730. They married on 10 July 1751 by licence and their marriage would have been subject to the newly introduced 'Law of Marriage'. Previously marriages could take place anywhere as long as the service was performed by a member of the clergy. The change in the law stated that ceremonies must be held in a church to ensure parental consent had been given and to avoid bigamy. I managed to find their children, twelve in total, two of which died very young and included **James**, our gt x 4 grandfather. The children were Thomas, Samuel (i) who died at three months, John, Ann, Richard, Elizabeth, Sarah, Margaret (i) who died at five, Samuel (ii), Margaret (ii), William and Mary. By the time Margaret (ii) was born, the family had relocated from Adlestrop to Evenlode, in Gloucestershire. James was born when Richard had reached the grand age of forty-nine.

The poem in Adlestrop parish church:

Adlestrop

I remember Adlestrop –
The name, because one afternoon
Of heat the express-train drew up there
Unwontedly. It was late June

The steam hissed. Someone cleared his throat
No one left and no one came
On the bare platform. What I saw
Was Adlestrop—only the name

And willows, willow-herb and grass,
And meadowsweet, and haycocks dry,
No whit less still and lonely fair
Than the high cloudlets in the sky

And for that minute a blackbird sang
Close by, and round him, mistier,
Farther and farther, all the birds
Of Oxfordshire and Gloucestershire

Edward Thomas

Images from the lovely little parish Church at Adlestrop, home to so many Tidmarshes whose lives were interwoven with this place.

Level 6 (part) and Level 7 (part), 1770–1797

Evenlode

Evenlode is a small, quiet village to the south-east of Adlestrop, mentioned in the Domesday Book as having ten households and where the family located to around 1770. Four of **Richard and Merrell's** children were born here—Margaret (ii), William, Mary and James. If Churchill was a typical Cotswold village, for me Evenlode is just special. It doesn't have the amount of Tidmarsh traffic as Adlestrop but there is definitely something special about this little church. It saw four baptisms and one marriage. I was convinced that the baptism font was the original but was kindly bought back to reality by my cousin who doubted it was. However,

I think the original font would have been in that location, which is good enough for me.

St Edward's Parish Church.

Anyway, back to **James**, my gt x 4 grandfather, who was born in 1773 and at the age of twenty-four, married **Mary Edens** from the tiny hamlet of Fawler, Oxfordshire at St Marys and All Saints Church in Charlbury on 19 February 1797. Within three years of getting married they had moved out of Evenlode and commenced the journey to Oxfordshire, by way of Fawler and the village of Stonesfield.

West Oxfordshire—The Return

Levels 7, 8 and 9, 1797–1859

James and Mary moved around several times. They had six children, three girls and three boys. Their first son, **Thomas**, my gt x 3 grandfather, was born in Stonesfield in 1799 (more of Stonesfield later). Their second son, John, was born in 1802 in the hamlet of Salford which is located 1.5 miles outside of Chipping Norton. They then seemed to settle for a while in Fawler, a lovely hamlet and the family home of the Edens, sheltered in the valley of the river Evenlode, 1.5 miles south-east of Charlbury, where their third son Richard was born in 1804, also their daughters Anne in 1805, Elizabeth in 1811 and Jane in 1814. As significant in our family tree as this hamlet is, it's very unassuming and seems to have missed the Cotswold tourist trails, so maybe it's just lucky. It was certainly lucky for the Tidmarsh family as two of its matriarchs came from there.

This story will focus now on **Thomas,** who was born in Stonesfield in 1799. He worked as an agricultural labourer and married **Martha Brooks**, from the village of Fawler (Fawler again), in the parish church of Charlbury on 7 April 1828.

Stonesfield and the larger nearby village of Charlbury are very close together and have a rich history of Tidmarsh families.

Stonesfield was our first family history destination, mentioned in the Domesday Book of 1086 as having eight households. Although this is not where the family story started, it was our first stop. We decided to follow Audrey's trail, which reached as far as **James** and **Mary** who we knew were buried in the churchyard here. It's a small, quiet place, once famous for its slate mining and the wonderful thirteenth-century Church of St James the Great, which even has its own 'lock-up'. Behind the 'lock-up' is the former site of a glove factory, one of many in the area at the time where many of the Tidmarsh women worked, now converted into a nursery school. We were given access to the parish archives, not yet relocated to the main county archive in Oxford, luckily for us.

Stonesfield

Location within Oxfordshire

High Street and thirteenth-century lock-up, note the Stonesfield slate roofs and Cotswold stone walls.

St James the Great Parish Church.

Arrival.

Church post card.

Searching their archives, a wonderful start to my journey.

Researching in the vault.

Karen and Lindsey.

Archive document.

Grave of Reuben and Elizabeth.				The 'old guard'.

This visit was bitter-sweet, as even though we knew **James and Mary** were buried here, there were no grave plot references to be found. However, we did find James' brother Reuben and his wife Elizabeth. On plot A24, an imposing granite cross stands over the grave that contains them both. At this point, the search for ancestors becomes real as one moves from researching books and the internet to actually touching a piece of family history.

Thomas Snr and Martha had seven children, most of whom were buried in Charlbury, where there is a high concentration of Tidmarsh clans. But from this point, things start to get challenging.

By looking at the censuses and archive documents around this time, the household contained ten children. Upon further investigation, it appears there were three children which were not Thomases but were living with him under his guardianship. The children were Jane b.1828, Eliza b.1850, the illegitimate daughter of Jane, William b.1830 (see note), Fanny b.1832, James b.1834,

John b.1844, Reuben b.1845, my Gt x 2 Grandmother **Mary** b.1839, Ann, the illegitimate daughter of Mary b.1854 and **Thomas**, my gt grandfather, the illegitimate son of Mary b.1859.

Here, the story takes one of two interesting turns—Mary decides to keep the Tidmarsh surname for both of her children. Both were illegitimate, neither took on her new surname. Ann remained within her grandmother's household; Thomas is another story. At this point our surname could have become Stayte.

There is a little confusion here with Ann. The parish records have her birth date as 1854, five years before the birth of Thomas, yet they were both baptised in 1859, which would indicate that they could be twins. Ann was further confirmed in 1870, but is registered in the census of 1871 as being part of the household of Mary and her new husband, Frederick Stayte with a birth date of 1854 which makes her five years older than her brother but baptised at the same time. There is also a gap in the history of **Thomas (Jnr)**. He didn't live with his mother and stepfather, neither did he seem to remain part of the Thomas and Martha household, yet reappears in London in his teens. I have made some conjectures later on but I am trying to find out what happened in the ten years between his mother remarrying when he was six and him reappearing in east London at sixteen.

Note: A little unpleasant anecdote about William, from the *Banbury Guardian*, Thursday, 6 June 1850:

> 'Assault—James Griffin and William Tidmarsh, young men of Stonesfield, were charged with having on the 27th May, at that parish, assaulted Caroline Hannah Barrett, a young woman of that place. Tidmarsh did not appear to his summons.'

> From the evidence given, both of them, in their twenties, desisted when being told to by the victim. In court James Griffin, having used no force, was free to go. Our William, however, after causing a minor injury to the victim incurred

the displeasure of the magistrate. 'The Magistrates intimated their displeasure at Tidmarsh's conduct by convicting him with a 5s fine and 10s 6d in costs and in default of payment, 14 days imprisonment.'

When **Thomas (Snr)** died, he was buried at St James the Great on 29 September 1847 at the age of forty-eight and Martha then became head of the household until she remarried, to a man named William Panting. She died in October 1892 at the age of eighty-three, outliving her new husband William by twenty-eight years and was buried in Chipping Norton rather than Charlbury, which is where all of Thomas and Martha's children, with the exception of Reuben are buried. Which takes us now to the larger nearby village of Charlbury.

Charlbury

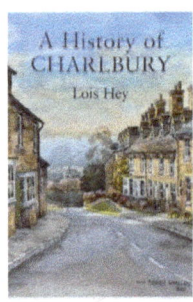

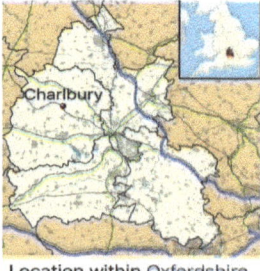

Location within Oxfordshire

A charming market town, on the edge of Wychwood Forest and the Cotswolds, home to generations of various branches of the Tidmarsh family. Here we visited the parish Church of St Mary's and All Saints to meet with Leah, the Charlbury archivist and the lovely volunteers that run the village museum, open on Saturdays from 10:00–12:00, entrance admission being the princely sum of £1, bargain!

We know that **Mary Tidmarsh** lived here, it's likely that her daughter Ann lived with Martha for a while but her son **Thomas** is more of a mystery as he disappears from the household during his younger years until he appears again in east London.

Church of St Mary's and All Saints

A fairly unimposing church, yet well-appointed and modernised, with an extensive community presence, dating back to the twelfth century and built on the site of an old Saxon Church. Beautiful twelfth-century rounded arches combine with the more pointed design favoured in the thirteenth century and there's an amazing spiral staircase leading up to the bell tower. However, there's an even more amazing graveyard, but many of the Tidmarsh graves are unreadable.

Lined up in front of the Church of St Mary's and All Saints, Charlbury, a wall of Tidmarsh gravestones.

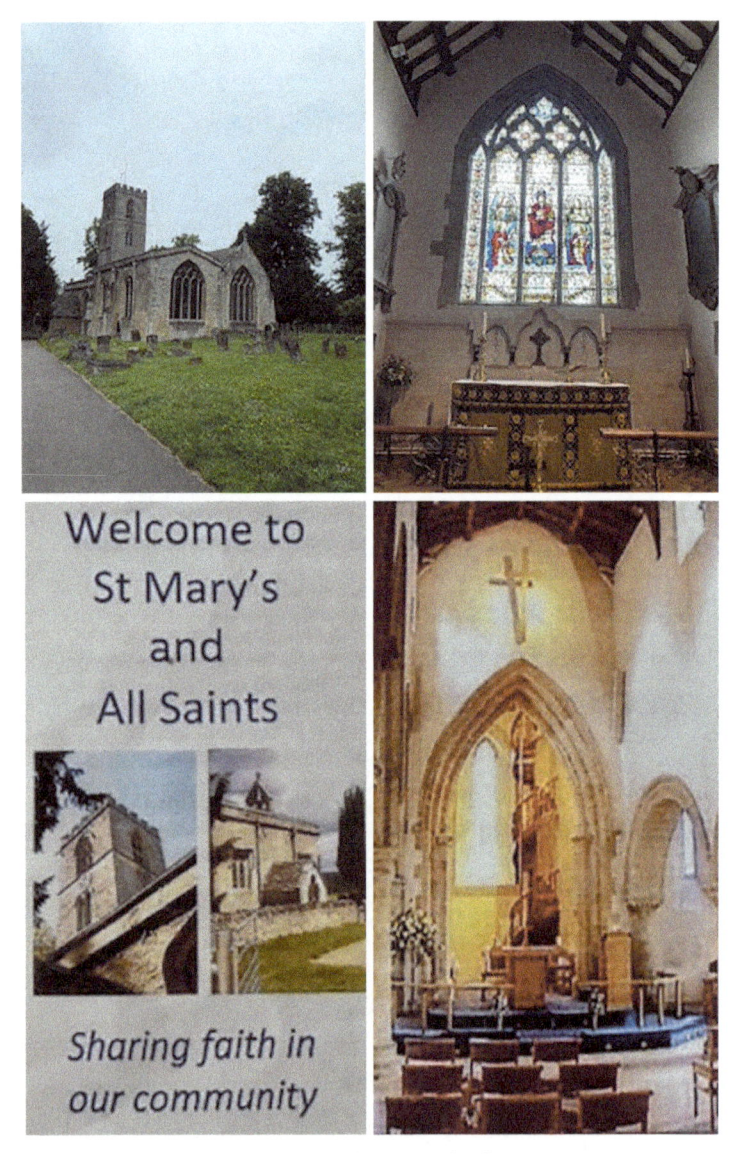

St Mary's and All Saints, Charlbury.

THE TIDMARSH FAMILY TREE

A Tidmarsh among the Tidmarshes—six Tidmarsh graves, five adults and one child.

As in Adlestrop, there are many Tidmarsh and Tidmarsh-related graves, but most are unreadable. Nearly all of our gt x 3 uncles and aunts are buried here. Again, as in Adlestrop, the map of grave plots is sadly lacking detail from that period of time, so there's a lot of guessing involved.

Charlbury Museum

The museum, open Saturday mornings, run by volunteers.

The card archive system—simple but effective.

One of the best small village museums in England I've ever visited, probably because I have a family association with the village but nevertheless, a treasure trove of local history. There are some examples of the gloves that were made in Charlbury and surrounding areas that became world famous. We were allowed access to four long metal drawer boxes, containing records of births, baptisms, deaths and burials going back 500 years. With so many Tidmarshes, Titmarshes and Tydemarshes it's a challenge to define the right Thomas, John or James, but some direct line Tidmarshes were found and we also discovered a Tidmarsh family house and the lane that **Mary** lived in.

So, to recap this section of the family—**Mary** is a pivotal figure and the reason we retained the Tidmarsh surname. She had two children out of wedlock, Ann and **Thomas Jnr,** my gt. grandfather, who both retained the Tidmarsh surname as the father/s of both children are unknown. We can confirm that the census of the time puts Ann within the custodianship of her grandmother, Martha, and her second husband, William Pantin. Thomas, however, may well have been looked after by relatives as this period is a grey area as far as he is concerned. My personal view is that Martha's household was rather congested. Her husband had died, leaving her as head of the household, Ann had been taken in but Thomas was probably too much and either stayed with Mary and her new husband (there is no evidence for this), or with Martha and her new husband (there is no evidence for this either), or, more likely, handed to relatives to live within their guardianship. I think it was with these relatives that he made the move south.

Mary married Frederick Henry Stayte in Charlbury on 14 October 1865 and died in 1926 at the age of eighty-seven. She was buried in Charlbury and this is the grave I was most looking forward to finding, but unfortunately, I had no luck. Mary and Frederick had ten children together but only four survived— George b.1868, Lizzie Selina b.1869, Lettie b.1870 and Rosa b.1872, a busy four years.

Tidmarsh household, in Sheep St. Ironically in-between a pub and a Methodist chapel.

This small road used to be called Back Lane, where Mary Tidmarsh and Frederick Stayte lived.

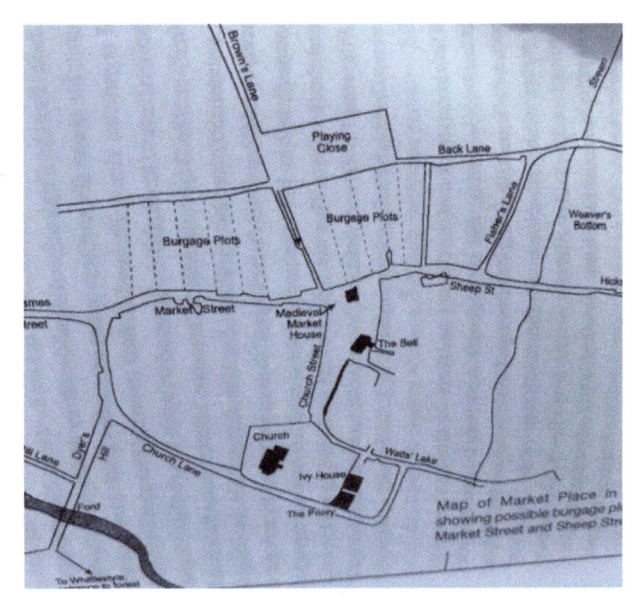

Charlbury nineteenth-century street map;
Tidmarshes were in Sheep St. and Back Lane.

The picturesque entrance to St Mary's that has seen baptisms,
marriages and burials of Tidmarsh's since the seventeenth century.

Oxfordshire to East London

The Journey of Thomas
Level 10 (part), 1859

I know that **Thomas (Jnr)**, my gt grandfather, was born in 1859 in Stonesfield, the illegitimate son of **Mary**, daughter of **Thomas (Snr).** However, he does not appear in the names of people present in **Thomas and Martha's** household by his teenage years, but does appear in London as part of the household of a Samuel Tidmarsh, who I suspect was an uncle or distant relative. So, the first mystery I came across is the reason for leaving Oxfordshire. It's not certain but it may well have been the lure of work in London in the newly built Victoria Dock, rather than the agricultural labouring that most of the Tidmarsh families in that area were involved in. Or, he could have travelled with the family he was staying with when they relocated because he had nowhere else to go. I often wonder what happened to him in those lost ten years.

From the rolling hills and valleys of agricultural Oxfordshire ...
London at the time of Thomas's arrival.

Level 10 (part) and Level 11, 1885–1919

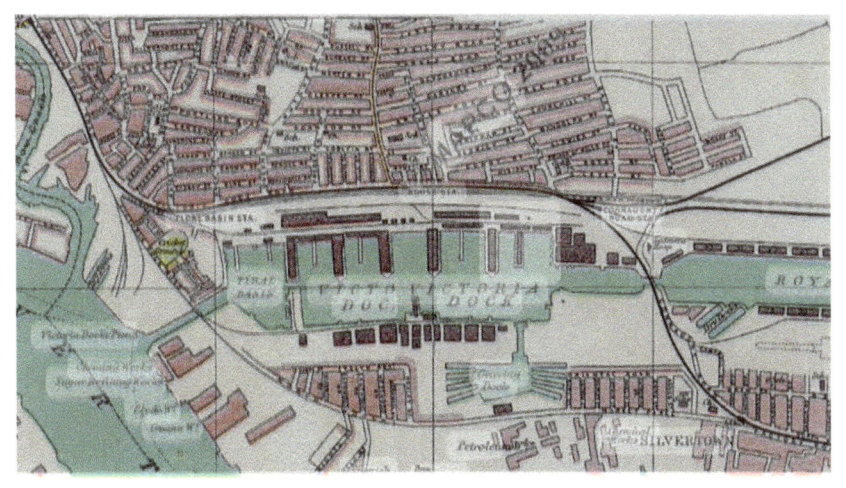

The new Victoria Dock.

During this period, trading in London was chaotic. The river was congested, road and rail networks were poor and plundering was an everyday occurrence. During the 1800s a group of industrialists and entrepreneurs decided to build a dock that was bigger and deeper than anything seen before. By 1880, these docks were so successful that they were expanded and 1885 saw the completion of Victoria Dock, the largest of the three new docks built in east London at that time and the first built to accommodate steamships. From out of the Essex marshlands to the east of London, industrialisation and the opportunity for traders to dock steamships on a quick turnaround created thriving multi-cultural communities, drawing labour from abroad and the rural regions, providing work for the newly arrived Thomas Tidmarsh, as well as the Woodward family (more of them later).

Victoria docks—early image (*stock photos c/o Wikipedia*).

It was here that **Thomas** started work. By sixteen we know that he was resident in the West Ham area and employed as a docker, but it's likely he started work at a younger age.

Before **Thomas** married my gt grandmother, **Florence**, he was married to an Irish girl called Sarah Flanagan. I use the term married guardedly as it was inferred on Sarah's death certificate. She was described as 'wife of Thomas Tidmarsh' and the certificate was marked with an 'X' as the mark of Thomas Tidmarsh, with the description under his mark as 'widower of the deceased'. However, I have been unable to find a marriage certificate so this may be just a generic term used to protect her reputation and the reputation of her children.

Born in 1862, Sarah's family originated from County Cork before moving to Fulham where she worked as a general servant. She had two daughters by **Thomas**, Florence b.1883 in Fulham and Lily Maud b.1887, in Plaistow. Lily Maud did not survive birth and died from convulsions. Sarah died ten days later on 14 February 1887 of 'puerperal mania' and TB.

Here is another family twist—if Sarah Flanagan had survived and remained married to Thomas, none of the family lines that we know would exist. There would be a Tidmarsh line, but it wouldn't be us.

Sarah was buried on 18 February 1887 in West Ham cemetery, in a public grave, as is her daughter Lily: at the far north-west end of the cemetery, section N, plot 37 for Sarah and plot 33 for Lily. Being a public grave, many bodies are in each of the plots and there are no headstones. The records for public graves are scarce, so what you see in the photos is a 'best guess', but they are there somewhere. A very poignant moment for me, I'm not sure exactly why. It was a long search but worth every second.

The area containing the burial plots of Sarah Flanagan and Lily Maud Tidmarsh.

Sarah's surviving daughter Florence b.1883 married Walter Sylvester Day in 1904, when she was twenty-one. They had one child, Florence b.1909. She died at the age of fifty-eight in 1941 and is buried in the City of London Cemetery, square 401, number 109656, Walter outlived her, dying at the age of ninety-five in 1978. They are buried together. Their daughter Florence married

Charles Ranton b.1882. Charles died in 1972, Florence outlived him by twenty years and died in 1993. They are both buried in Southend. I don't know how much contact, if any, her father **Thomas** had with Florence as she was only four when Sarah died. As a single working man, recently bereaved of a wife and child, it's likely that she was looked after by other Tidmarsh family members. Thomas married **Florence Woodley** in the same year so she may have been taken in by them until her teens, she doesn't appear as a member of his household in any of the censuses.

Florence Woodley was born in 1869 in the West Ham area of east London. She married **Thomas** in 1887 at St Luke's Church, Victoria Docks (what now is Canning Town). St Luke's was heavily damaged during WWII and was deconsecrated in the 1960s. It avoided demolition though and is now used as a community centre.

The Canning Town area, where the Woodleys, east London Tidmarshes and Woodwards (my grandmother's family) lived, was fast becoming a bastion of industrial development with a multi-cultural community as a result of the influx of labour to feed the new factories and docks.

The first workers' homes built in Canning Town around 1850.

Workers' housing.

THE TIDMARSH FAMILY TREE

Bidder Street in 1891, one of the oldest parts of Canning Town. The Bidder Street area is now an industrial area

Street scene.

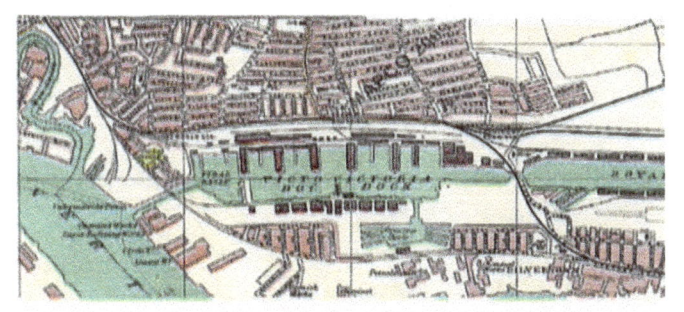

Map 1908, showing Canning Town to the north of Royal Victoria Dock and Silvertown to the south of the dock.

Victoria Dock early map.

St Luke's Church.

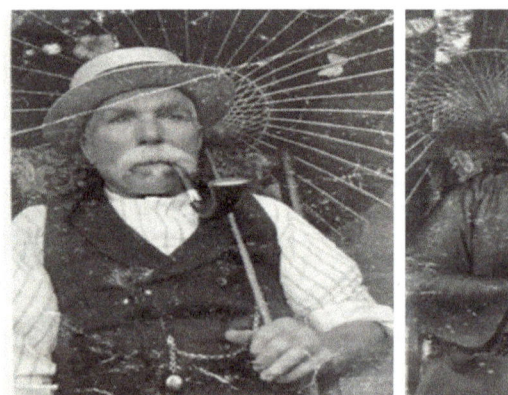

Thomas and Florence Tidmarsh.

The children of Thomas and Florence: Tilley b.1889, Edith Alice (Aunt Doll) b.1890, William Thomas b.1892, **George Harry** b.1894, Nellie b.1896, Frederick Charles b.1903.

    Another mystery I came across was Cicilia (Cecilia) Parkin. The 1911 census tells us that here was an adopted girl of this name in Thomas and Florence's household. She was eighteen months old, so probably born in 1909 in Battersea. In 1911, the term 'adopted' was a generic description for someone being 'looked after'.

The laws of adoption were created in 1926 and adoption as we know it started on 01 Jan 1927. This makes it very hard to track Cicilia as she doesn't stay within Thomas's household for long and could well have changed her surname. She would have been eighteen when the adoption laws were introduced so she may well remain a mystery. I still wonder where she came from and where she went. I often research her and have come close but nothing definite.[3]

Interestingly, on the same census my grandfather is named as Henry, sixteen years old, occupation labourer. At this time the family were living at two Bengoe Street, Tidal Basin, West Ham. The census states Thomas and Florence were married for twenty-three years, had a total of seven children, six alive and one that had died. I have assumed that Cecilia is not included, as an adopted child, and that Thomas misread the instructions and included his two children with Sarah—hence six children alive (George, his siblings and Florence) and the deceased Lily.

Soon after that census, the household moved from east to south-east, when they moved from West Ham to Charlton, where they resided at 12 Atlas Gardens, a small side road off of Hope and Anchor Road.

William Thomas, my Great Uncle Tom, died in 1923 in Dartford as a result of a traffic accident, which was an alleged suicide, and was buried in Charlton Cemetery. The story here is that he was in love with my grandmother and became suicidal when rejected.

Thomas died in 1926 and is buried in the same grave as his son Thomas, along with **Florence**, who died in 1935. When Florence died, it left the family with a problem—a forty-five-year-old Edith Alice (also known as Doll), who was incapable of looking after herself. More of her further on.

---

[3] On 25 August 1928, a Cecilia Parkin was married to Harold Edward Wright (1905–1973) in Paddington. This Cecilia was born in 1909, so nineteen years old, born in Wandsworth (within 2 miles of Battersea). Her mother was unknown and her father Thomas Parkin (spelt Partin on the marriage certificate) was deceased.

I'm not sure of the strength of the relationship between Thomas and George. I think there was a strong bond between George's brother Thomas as he was buried in the same plot as his parents. There are stories in the family that George didn't think highly of his father. Indeed, on George's marriage certificate, his father is named as William Thomas, the name of his brother. This could well have been a mistake by the clerk or even George, getting names confused, hardly surprising as he was on a forty-eight-hour pass and soon to return to the war. Or, it could well be that the relationship had broken down so much that he was ignored.

Thomas died at the age of sixty-seven, he would have been fifty-eight when George was wounded. I wonder what his feelings were, or if he was even aware.

Charlton cemetery. Resting place of Thomas, Florence and William Thomas. The grave was found through the efforts of my cousins, who along with one of my brothers have been caring for it ever since.

'In loving memory of William Thomas eldest son of Thomas and Florence Tidmarsh accidently killed at Dartford 31st July 1923 aged 31. A loving son a brother dear forever in our thoughts. Also Thomas Tidmarsh father of the above who passed away 6th July 1926 aged 68 years. The loved are never forgotten. Also of his wife Florence Tidmarsh who died 17th June 1935 aged 66 years. Dearly Loved.'

London

Level 11, 1894–1989

George and Daisy

It's impossible to write enough about these two in a few paragraphs. Fair to say that all of their grandchildren have fond memories of them and George has a story (well, probably a few) of bravery that is worthy of respect and admiration and also has a remarkable tale of bad luck. The narrative from now will refer to them as George and Daisy, although to me, like my cousins, they are simply 'Nanny and Grandad'.

I intended to give a brief overview of their lives, similar to that of my other ancestors, except that I was there for a big part of it, so my memories and interests run a lot deeper. Once you start a piece like this, it's difficult to know where to stop and this family history started to evolve into something focussed on my grandfather. The reason for this, in my opinion, is that he is the person who links past, present and future. He is the result of the tumultuous times and adventures of our ancestors, and at the same time is the example by which his grandchildren try and live their lives. So, hereunder is a resume of the 'level 11' generation, but further on I'll delve deeper into his short but eventful army experience and life after WWI. This is by no means a comprehensive memoir, but hopefully I have included enough to build a sufficient picture. I have given George and Daisy separate chapters.

Level 12, 1919–present

The children of George and Daisy, subject to another narrative when the times comes, I hope:

Frederick George (Fred) b.1919, d.2010, who married Ida Joan Notman b.1924, d.2005.
Harry William Thomas b.1921, d.2010, who married Patricia Mary Parlour b.1920, d.2014.
Kenneth William (Ken) b.1928, d.2020, who married Audrey Eileen Taylor b.1927, d.2010.
Reginald Stanley (Reg) b.1930, who married Doreen Rose Howard b.1932.
Barbara May b.1937, d.2020, who married Ronald Sydney Tame b.1933, d.2010.

Fred, Harry, Ken and Reg.

Barbara

Fred was named after George's brother, and his second name was George after his father. Harry was named after George's second name, and his second names, William Thomas, after George's elder brother—before the falling out.

George Harry Tidmarsh

I wrote a poem many years ago about George's experiences in WWI (or what I imagined his experience to be) and sub-titled it 'The story of George, or Harry, or maybe George' as there was a time when he didn't know what his first name was. His parents referred to him as Harry, even Henry. The question was settled when Florence dug his birth certificate out of a large trunk, when it was requested by the army on enlistment, only for him to find that he was officially a George. I have used this name to remain consistent. The fourth child and second son to **Thomas** and **Florence,** born in West Ham on 10 August 1894, the same year as the opening of Tower Bridge to traffic, to give some context.

George, like his father, worked as a dock labourer and then a print press operator, before enlisting in the army at twenty. He joined the Kings Royal Rifles on 4 November 1915 in Greenwich and was despatched to the Training Reserve in Winchester, one Private Tidmarsh, Harry, A211548. He served in northern France and Belgium where he was granted leave to travel back to England to marry his fiancé Daisy Woodward, which he did on 19 May 1917, after receiving special dispensation to get married on a Sunday. He quickly rejoined the regiment in Ypres, where he was involved in what is referred to as the Third Battle of Ypres, otherwise known as the First Battle of Passchendaele, where he was badly wounded. He was taken by stretcher to a field hospital, likely by volunteers from the Salvation Army (more about them later). From the field hospital or dressing station he was transferred to Le Tréport military hospital, where he spent thirteen months in recovery (more of this later). During this time his new wife, Daisy, travelled to Le Tréport along with many other army wives, to attend their husbands. After a long, drawn-out period in hospital he was returned home to England. He was officially discharged on 8 October 1918 and received his silver war badge, B47335, which designated him as an injured serviceman, along with a Victory medal and WWI British war medal. Limited to the sort of work he could do due to his injuries, he became a hospital porter, a job that he loved and one he pursued until retirement. His return home from his horrendous experience in Belgium and northern France meant that, although disabled, he was alive and able to return to his new wife and soul mate and to start the next phase of his life, which commenced in the following year with the arrival of a son, Frederick George.

Upon his return from Le Tréport military hospital in France, George and Daisy lived at sixteen Rainton Road, Charlton, before moving to 111 Moorside Road, Downham which my father remembers as having an amazing view over Downham Fields towards the city. Mind you, he had to clamber over a wall and up a tree first. To those who know my father, this will not come as a surprise. From Moorside Road, the family moved into the large, double-fronted house that I remember from childhood—1 King Alfred Avenue, Bellingham SE6, but more of this house and its memories later.

In a little over twenty years, the world would be plunged into war yet again, George would have been forty-five and working as a hospital porter, his eldest child Fred would have been twenty, the youngest, Barabara, only two. Only Fred would have seen service, the other boys evacuated during six years of turmoil. Those years and the years that follow will be the subject of another story.

On the year George was born, Tower Bridge was opened for traffic by Edvard VII. The year he died saw the fall of the Berlin Wall.

Daisy Woodward

Daisy was born on 3 June 1896 in Silvertown, east London, one of seven children. She was baptised on 24 June of the same year at St Mark's Church, Victoria Docks. Like the neighbouring St Luke's Church in Victoria Docks, where Thomas and Florence were married, it survived WWII but was deconsecrated in the 1960s due to falling numbers as a result of the slum clearances happening at the time. It's now the site of the Brick Lane Music Hall. Her father, Lewis Woodward b.1862 was originally from Southampton and her mother, Leah b.1867 was originally from the Isle of Wight. According to the research I've done so far, Daisy's Grandmother b.1836, was originally from County Cork and after leaving Ireland for east London, became head of the household after the death of Daisy's Grandfather Anthony when her father was only nine. The Woodwards were a dockland family, living in Silvertown. Lewis was a lighterman, a big, strong man according to my grandmother, who, when they were small would arrive home on payday and slap his wage packet on the table so that Leah could take what she needed. Daisy's family originated in Hampshire, centred around Southampton and Winchester, before her father, Lewis, moved from Southampton to Silvertown. Daisy had six siblings; all the girls being named after flowers: Lewis b.1885, Phillip b.1867, William b.1891, Flora b.1892, Rose b.1901 and Lilly b.1904. I have traced Daisy's family back to the seventeenth century, to her gt x 4 grandparents, William and Ann (see Woodward family tree).

There is a possibility of a German, possibly Jewish connection in the Woodward family, which I will come to later.

I think I would be correct in saying that Daisy could be somewhat of a formidable woman, similar to many women living and bringing up a family in post-war Britain, not least because she had four boys to deal with before her first and only daughter. There is a thought that, had Barbara arrived before the boys, there may well have been fewer boys!

She loved cleaning! Everything in King Alfred Ave seemed to be spotless. She was also on the cleaning rota of Bellingham Congregational Church, where I was baptised, and I recall at her funeral, the minister (I think it was Rev. Hughes-Riley) talking about her energy and the time when he ended a conversation with her by saying 'God Bless', to which she replied 'He does!'

I think the endearing memory for many of us would be her energy and her ability to ground George when he became too 'knowledgeable' on a subject. The phrase 'flipping Tidmarshes—flipping know-it-alls' will stay with me forever, but so will the smile that came with it and George's laughter. Even he knew when he'd met his match.

She regularly went to neighbouring Catford to do her shopping, often regaling shopkeepers with the difference in price between their produce and their competitors. When informing a butcher that sausages were cheaper in Kennedy's, the butcher kindly suggested she may prefer to buy them there then. Her enthusiasm for the Catford trips didn't diminish even after she was mugged by two young gentlemen and had her wrist broken whilst struggling with them to retain her handbag. All the way to Belgium to nurse wounded soldiers, only to be robbed in Catford.

I will return to George and Daisy as a couple, because that's what they were, but the Tidmarsh family tree would not bear the same quality of fruit were it not for this wonderful, dynamic woman.

My cousin recalls: 'I always remember being on the bus from Lewisham to Bromley with Mum, when Nanny got on at Catford. She had been shopping and got off at Bellingham Station to walk back up the hill with her shopping. She must have been fit because that was a long steep hill.'

My father tells a story about his brother Ken measuring the quality of Daisy's dinners by the amount of Rennies that would be needed as a result. A great source of amusement to his brothers, but all out of earshot I suspect.

Another food-related Daisy anecdote is that her next-door neighbour (whose garden was always untidy, unlike Daisy's which was always pristine) kept a greyhound in the garden. Dad tried to convince her that greyhounds should have their ribs showing, a theory that she disagreed with, hence her sneaking out to feed it!

I mentioned that she was very keen on cleaning. The house was always spotless and she was 'always washing curtains and scrubbing her step and path', as my cousin recalls. In her kitchen was a large blue cooker, the type with a plate rack on top. Daisy cleaned this cooker regularly, almost religiously, every week, because that was in her nature. My cousin recalls: 'For those that don't remember, Nan had a cooker which was blue and white enamel. She used to soak the elements in soda water every Sunday and it was pristine. The British Gas company took her cooker for their museum when they went into the home. Amazing.' Some of my cousins went on a quest to find it, even receiving a response from the museum curator and it may also have featured in a period TV programme. Very few historical narratives will feature a cooker, but I suspect Daisy would be justly proud that her grandchildren are paying homage to her hard work.

One of the most interesting things I found out when researching Daisy are possible German and Jewish connections. My cousin Kay was told that Daisy's family, most likely her grandparents or great grandparents, fled Germany to come to England and anglicised their name, replacing the V's with W's. The family research that I've done of the Woodward family show her parents originating in the Southampton area and her grandparents from Southampton and Co. Cork (see the Woodward family tree), but that may just be the 'official' version, or the place they resettled when entering the country. There is a suggestion that Daisy's parents were Jewish, which is more than likely, but I have no evidence yet of that.

When Daisy died in 1988, she had been married to George for seventy-one years. They died within a year of each other as though George realised that there was little left to live for after she had gone. They ended their days in a small room in a nice care home, a million miles away from the warmth and fun of one King Alfred Ave. Daisy suffered a stroke just before her death and was never the same afterwards, but to George, I suspect, she never changed.

Daisy's parents, Leah and Lewis Woodward.

Bellingham Congregational Church. This building plays a central part in the London Tidmarsh family history. I include this photo because Daisy cleaned here, George and Daisy worshipped here, Daisy's funeral was here, my parents were married here and probably some of my uncles and my aunt. I was baptised here (maybe some of my cousins were also).

The building at the rear housed the famous 'Congo Club' where my father met my mother, at least one of my uncles met his wife and my mother's brother and sister met their spouses.

Opposite Bellingham Congregational in Bellingham Green, there's a CoE church, St Dunstan's. My father Reg and his friend Keith Taylor (my aunty Audrey's brother) used to pump the organ for services on Sunday morning. One day, when I was a child, we were driving home from Nanny's house and Dad stopped the car outside St Dunstan's, got out, went up to the church for what seemed like ages and then returned smiling. When he was a boy, he wrote his name with privet hedge leaves on the church wall and he wanted to see if it was still there! Gotta love that guy.

Bellingham Congregational church and the famous 'Congo Club'.

No other reason for including this photo, except for that smile.

The Great War 1914–1918

Four years when the world changed

The great war to end all wars, that gave a whole new meaning to the word horror, four years of chaos, confusion, death and destruction, that ended empires and saw the first real use of trench warfare and the creation of 'new volunteer armies' that saw the enlistment and near fatal involvement of my grandfather.

The King's Royal Rifle Corps During WWI

'Swift and Bold'.

Introduction

George Tidmarsh, my grandfather, left his job as a lead press hand in Charlton in 1915 to enlist. I don't know the reason for his choice of regiment, but I would surmise that the infantry was a prime choice at the time for volunteers with few technical skills. The regiment he chose was the King's Royal Rifle Corps (KRR), enlisting in Greenwich on the 4 November 1915 at the age of twenty in their Training Corps. He was taken to join the KRR Training Reserve in Winchester to become A211548 Private Tidmarsh, Harry George (his birth certificate wasn't found until it was too late).

The Winchester barracks still houses the Regimental Museum, although the KRR is now amalgamated into other regiments, the most notable being the 'Royal Green Jackets'.

A Brief History

The King's Royal Rifle Corps was an infantry regiment of the British Army that was originally raised in British North America as the Royal American Regiment during what was known as the 'The French and Indian War' from 1754–1763. At this time my gt x 6 grandparents, Thomas and Margaret Tidmarsh, were smallholders in Gloucestershire and could well have been aware of that fact. Their gt x 5 grandson, however, would be fighting in KRR uniform in one of the bloodiest and costly wars ever known. The regiment served for more than 200 years throughout the British Empire before being amalgamated and eventually disbanded and absorbed into the Royal Green Jackets in 1966.

KRR Western Front areas of operation, 1915–1918

- 1915: Battle of the Hooge, Second Attack of Bellewaarde.
- 1916: Somme—The Battle of Delville Wood, the Battle of Flers-Courcelette.
- 1917: The German retreat to the Hindenburg Line, the First and Third Battle of the Scarpe at Arras, the Battle of Langemark, the First and Second Battles of Passchendaele.
- 1918: Somme—The Battle of St Quentin, the Battle of the Avre, where after huge casualties they were withdrawn from the frontline, reduced in number and disbanded on 3 August.

Western Front

The assassination of Archduke Franz Ferdinand, figurehead of the Austro-Hungarian Empire, by extremists in Serbia, a country recently annexed by them, led to a series of events that cast Europe and then the rest of the globe directly or indirectly into the first Great War. Germany's violation of Belgian borders caused Britain to honour its protection treaties with them and enter the war, although it was also thought to be the best way to defend and restore the balance of power in Europe and safeguard our position in the world, which was being overtaken by both the US and Germany. On the 28 June 1914, the spark in Serbia became a flame in Europe and the world fell into conflict. At that time, The Earl Kitchener became the secretary of state for war and foreseeing a long campaign ahead, started organising the biggest volunteer army that Britain had ever seen.

By late 1914, the Eastern and Western Fronts had opened up and the carnage had begun. To the West, the German advance had been halted by the British Expeditionary Forces, which resulted in both sides holding ground in preparation for a series of vicious and protracted battles in and around Ypres, the ancient Flemish city whose fortifications guarded the Channel ports.

George was drafted into the 9th (Service) Battalion, KRR. This battalion was raised at Winchester on 21 August 1914, still in its infancy when George joined. It was formed as part of Kitchener's first 'New Army' and became part of the initial British Expeditionary Force.

By May 1915 the battalion was in France, landing in Boulogne on 20 May 1915. They fought in 'The Action of Hooge' in July and were of the first British troops to experience flamethrowers! They were moved to the Somme in 1916 and were then involved in many battles, not least of which were the push towards the Hindenburg Line and the First and Second Battles of Passchendaele. Like all Battalions, they suffered heavy casualties, before moving back to the Somme in 1918, when they were taken off the front line and engaged in building a new defensive line to the rear.

Ironically, George was a talented boxer. My uncle Ken, in his memory 'water of life' recalls that he reached the final of his regiment's boxing tournament. Unfortunately, he lost. Had he won, he would have remained at camp in England.

A Wedding

His first posting came on 3 March 1917, where as a reservist he was called up to fight on the Western Front. The KRR were part of the push to the Hindenburg Line, forcing the German Army back from whence they came. George received permission to briefly return to England in May 1917 to get married. How far in advance this was planned I'm not sure. It may well be that plans were in place but the war got in the way. I guess war will do that. Anyway, he received his permission and after receiving further permission to marry on a Sunday, he married his fiancé Daisy Woodward on 19 May. We understand that he returned to France, possibly the next day, to return to his regiment, which by then were heading towards a small Belgian village called Passchendaele.

Passchendaele

'Squire nagged and bullied till I went to fight,
(Under Lord Derby's scheme). I died in hell –
(They called it Passchendaele). My wound was slight,
And I was hobbling back; and then a shell
Burst slick upon the duck-boards: so I fell
Into the bottomless mud, and lost the light

Excerpt from 'Memorial Tablet' by Siegfried Sassoon.

For someone sitting at a desk, writing about an event that happened over 100 years ago, it's difficult to comprehend exactly what it was like. George rarely mentioned the war to his grandchildren, most of our information comes from stories passed down to us by parents and uncles.

What we do know is that he was badly injured by machine gun fire whilst fighting in the trenches. We know that he was at Passchendaele and the timings of his return to France from England after his marriage to Daisy Woodward in May and his discharge from the army in October would put him at the Third Battle of Ypres, the First Battle of Passchendaele, which commenced on 12 October 1917. His unit formed part of the Royal Lincolnshire Regiment, probably as a reserve. The reserves went over the top of the trenches after the specialised, or battle-hardened troops were struggling or getting pushed back.

A description of the First Battle of Passchendaele by a battle-hardened regular, Alexandre Arnoux, who experienced battles all over the Western Front: 'I've never been in what I call a real battle, with the whole line moving forward and the reserves coming up all the time, I've never been in that' (*The First World War*, Huw Strachan).

George would have been in one of the waves of reserves that relentlessly charged enemy lines. After another brutal encounter, the line retreated and George returned to the British forward trench, but without his rifle, which was dropped during the chaos. Upon his return he was threatened with a court martial if he didn't retrieve his weapon. He retuned to the battlefield, stopped to assist a fallen soldier and was badly wounded by enemy machine gun fire. It was 27th October 1917 and for George, the war was over.

It's widely believed by the family that he was taken from the battlefield by stretcher bearers who were volunteers from the Salvation Army and taken to a field hospital or dressing station. According to his discharge papers, he was wounded in the left leg, left side and left arm. The result of his injuries was a permanently stiff leg.

He was posted to return to England on 29 March 1918 and officially discharged as unable to fight on 8 October 1918. His discharge entitled him to qualify for a war pension, the maximum allowed at the time was 40/- per week, reduced in accordance with the seriousness of injury. George was entitled to 22/- per week.[4]

Incidentally, when he enlisted, he agreed for his pay to be deducted by 6d per day to be sent to his mother, Florence.

---

[4] 40/- denotes forty shillings, the pre-decimal currency. One shilling is approx. 5p.

KRR Corps—photos from Passchendaele. *Courtesy of the Wartime Memories Project.*

It's hard to grasp the enormity of the horror and chaos of those days. Photos can't really do it justice, but I have used a selection from an excellent book called *Passchendaele 1917* by Chris McNab, I picked it up in a second-hand shop for £2.50 and would recommend it as a read to anyone interested in the fast-fading history of those years.

The entrance to Ypres. George may well have passed through here on his way north-east to Passchendaele. The city was obliterated, as were the forests surrounding it. The photo on the right is all that was left after the battles, empty, lifeless and broken.

Field dressing station.

British infantry line, note the desolation of the surroundings and the awful mud.

A duckboard track, east of Ypres, the only way to cope with the mud. It rained constantly for two weeks in August 1917.

Exhausted Australian soldiers, sheltering on higher ground where it was dryer during the First Battle of Passchendaele.

Field Hospital

The circumstances of George's injuries are unknown, although given the basic tactics of trench warfare it leaves little to the imagination. Charges usually led to massacres, although there is a story that he retreated unharmed from a charge, only to go back out into the field to retrieve his rifle and search for one of his friends and was injured by machine gun fire as a result. He was lucky to be rescued alive and would have been taken to a field hospital or dressing station for first response medical attention. Field hospitals

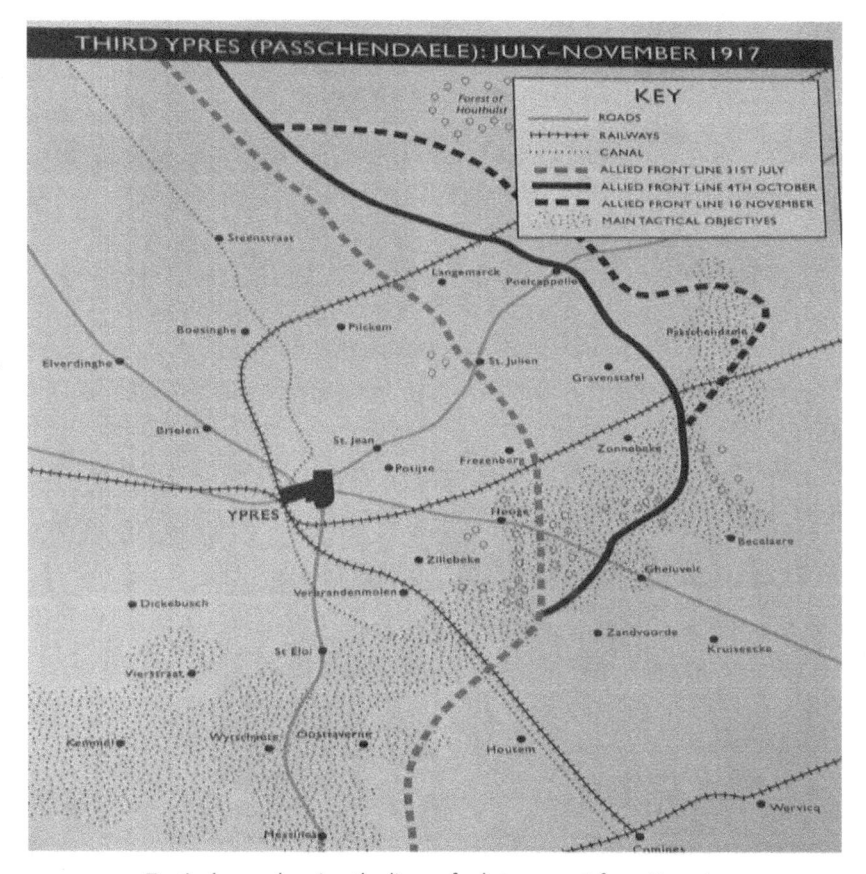

Tactical map showing the lines of advancement from Ypres to Passchendaele as the German Army was slowly pushed back.

on the Western Front were basic and the medical orderlies would only have time to perform urgent medical procedures, especially for badly wounded soldiers like George. As he explained it to me, 'They did what they could, but they didn't have the knowledge or skills at that time to do anything else.' I'm not sure how much medical attention was given to him in the field and not sure if that is where they stiffened his leg, however, his condition was serious, so he was transported to a purpose-built military hospital. It's also widely believed by the family that Daisy was allowed to visit him to act as a nurse whilst he recovered. It was common practice for wives to be taken over to military hospitals to assist with nursing and caregiving tasks. There's also a story about Daisy helping other wounded soldiers, including captured Germans, which, knowing my grandmother, I believe to be true. The military hospital he was transported to was at Le Tréport.

Le Tréport

Le Tréport is a French coastal town about 15 miles north-east of Dieppe. During WWI, when casualties were increasing at a frightening rate, it was necessary to set up a large, central hospital to try and cope. The Trianon Hotel Le Tréport was commandeered for this purpose. This imposing structure, near the cliffs overlooking the sea, would be home for George for the next thirteen months. The most important hospital centre on the Western Front, No.3 General Hospital, was established there in November 1914, No.16 General Hospital in February of 1915, No.2 Canadian General Hospital in March of 1915 and No.3 Convalescent Depot in June 1916. These hospitals contained nearly 10,000 beds. During WWII the hotel was destroyed by the German Army.

The hospital was formerly the Trianon Hotel, here seen in its full glory with overflow tents in the foreground.

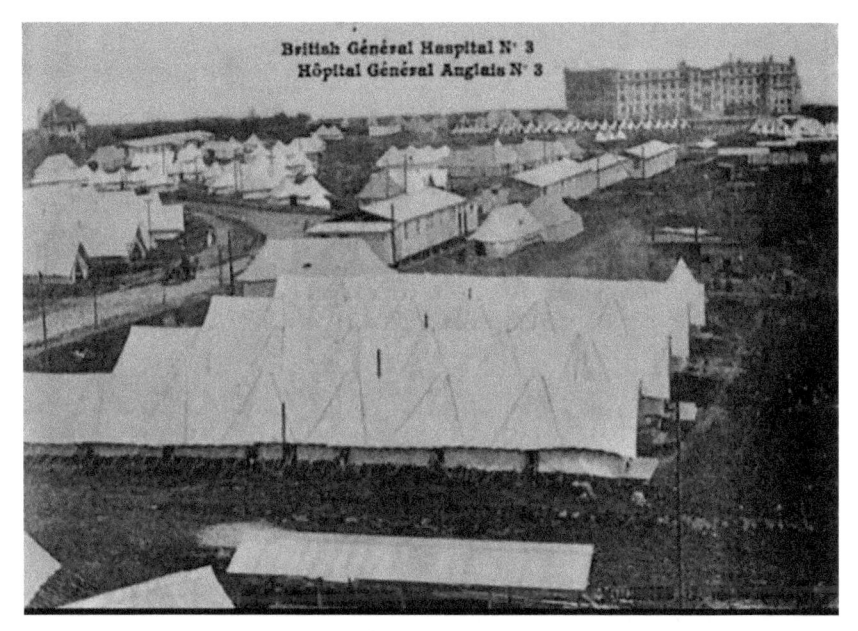

A view from further back giving an indication of just how huge this place was.

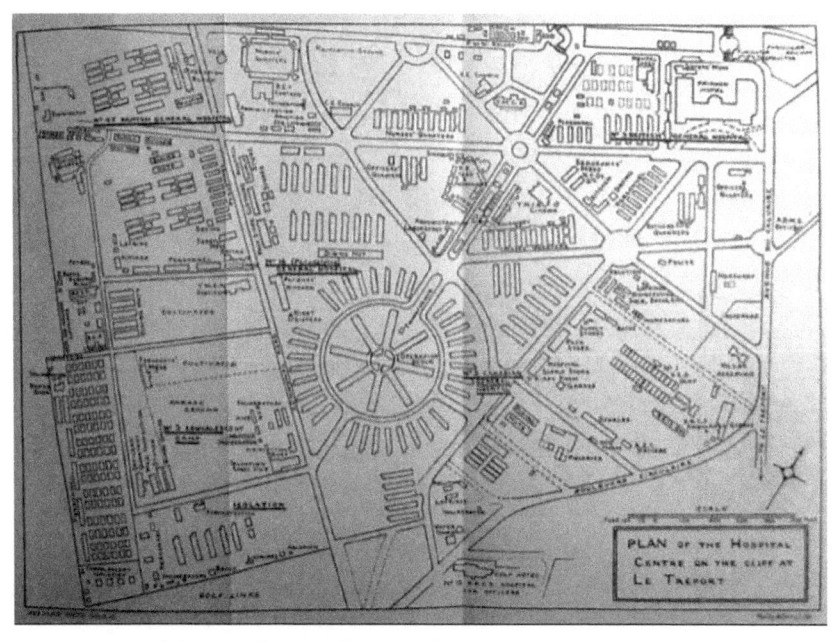

On plan, sprawling out like a small city, with nearly 10,000 beds.

Aftermath

The 'war to end all wars' ended on 11 November 1918, just one month after George returned home. The KRR saw action as a regiment and as part of the adapted 'New Army' units throughout northern France and Belgium, suffering horrendous casualties whilst participating in most of the strategic battles. The regiment received seven Victoria Crosses.

Two of my cousins visited the battlefields there some years ago, on a journey to see where it all happened, and kindly sent me these photos of the KRR regimental memorials.

Memorial to the fallen—KRR Museum, Winchester.

As for my grandad, on a personal level, I think the aftermath ran very deep. He rarely mentioned his wartime experiences. He never, as far as I am aware, mentioned Passchendaele in detail. He never showed his scars and never showed his tattoo to us grandchildren. I know from both my parents that they were told he was never the same after his return. He turned from extrovert to introvert, from outward facing to spiritual and reflective. He never wore his medals and never felt the need to seek appreciation or praise for what he went through. But then, who would be the same after what he saw?

George had the opportunity to become a Chelsea Pensioner[5] as an ex-soldier injured in service, once he reached the required age. He had no interest as he had no intention of being separated from Daisy. I also suspect he would never consider putting on another military uniform.

The Young Ones Depart

(The story of George, or Harry, or maybe George)
Full of bravado, the young ones depart
To the smoking, battle-scarred fields of north France
Fire in their bellies and fear in their hearts
To lay down their lives in the devil's great dance

Just twenty-one, leaving home and a wife
From a small London house far away
For king and for country, his struggle and strife
Against barrage of death's leaden spray

'Over the top lads, just one more push'
Came the officer's voice from behind
Through the thick sodden mud and parched broken bush
Came charging the youth of mankind

In the midst of the battle, a young man fell
Under the fire of burning spewed lead
From an enemy unknown, in his own private hell
May blame not be laid on his head

Coming too, now awake, in a large makeshift tent
With birdsong to replace battles' noise
Time to reflect and his sins to repent
Mind cast back to once carefree young joys

---

[5] Chelsea pensioners are residents of the Chelsea hospital retirement home for ex-soldiers or reside outside the hospital in other locations. Founded by Charles II, it's a care home for ex-servicemen who were injured in action or have over twenty years' service.

With body infested with man's manic spears
The surgeon worked on through the night
Whilst his wife traced her life through salt streams of tears
Then onward to ease others' plight

And so, through his spirit, his faith and his strength
The lonely young man, he slowly pulled through
Arm and body so scarred and leg stiffened full length
A part of the debt we all owe to the few

And a ceaseless reminder for following years,
as swaying red poppies will blanket those fields
That a cause can't be measured by rivers of
tears and the body gives in, but the heart never yields

And so goes the story, as I remember it told
From the small quiet man, nestled deep in his chair
Though your wounds may still weep and your body now old
Your courage and bravery dare Gods to compare

Now you are gone, more dreams to pursue
But your wit and your wisdom, our grandmother's laughter
Remain with us still, through memories soft hue
We'll never forget you, now or hereafter

Andrew Tidmarsh

Salvation Army

Most Saturdays, Mrs T and I venture down to the local Marks and Spencer food hall. Outside is an elderly, slightly built Salvation Army officer with her red plastic collection box and a handful of War Crys. In this increasingly cashless society, a collection box seems a little outdated, but I fold up a tenner and put it in regardless and ask the same question: 'Are we winning?' to which the answer is always, 'Yes, we have to.' (Memories of Daisy's response to the vicar at Bellingham.) Regardless of your opinion of the Salvation Army and their 'old fashioned' views on some subjects, I will always give and the reason is quite simple.

George was rescued from the battlefield by volunteer stretcher bearers from the Salvation Army. Their International Heritage Centre in London don't keep specific records of individual soldiers, but then there would have been too many to record properly. They did send me some 'War Cry' pages from the time describing their work to support both UK and US soldiers by providing stretcher and nursing services, driving ambulances and providing shelters for respite and spiritual care and food and clothing parcels.

These are a few of the photos they were kind enough to send me:

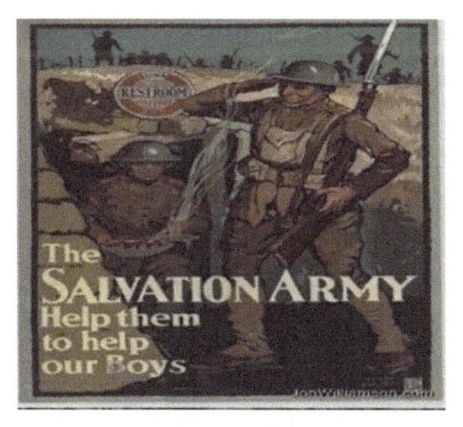

Propaganda.

Motorised ambulances soon replaced horses.

Scenes from the battlefields.

The reality—fighting through knee-high mud, finding a route around or sometimes through water-logged craters and barbed wire, unarmed and sitting targets. Some soldiers preferred fighting to stretcher bearing.

Stretcher bearing was not a pleasant job, it's no easy way to get out of conflict. It's hard, back-breaking work, under awful conditions. The mud at Passchedaele was knee high and made movement extremely difficult. In some parts of the Western Front, donkeys carrying ammunition would slip off of the duckboard paths and disappear into the mud! Not one square yard of ground was unscarred by the constant barrages, so there was no effective cover. Bearers had to work in tight, organised teams. Anyone who has carried a grown man on a stretcher knows just how hard it is. Then you need to manoeuvre through the deep, clinging mud and find a route through the bomb craters, by now full of water and the endless rows of barbed wire that would have been everywhere.

Chances are that as a volunteer your faith was leading you to serve your fellow man. In this case, their faith had led them into the mouth of hell. By the time they, hopefully, returned to the nearest trench or dressing station, they would be tired, caked in mud, with hands bleeding from pulling pieces of barbed wire from their clothing whilst on the move and all the time being a sitting target for the enemy, should they be so inclined to ignore your small badge with a red cross on it.

There are stories about soldiers who refused to be stretcher bearers. They would rather risk their lives in a charge than go though that.

George would have been resucued by a team of men similar to those in the picture (this was an actual rescue at Passchendaele) and taken to a dressing station or field hospital.

It was 1917, he was twenty-three, a newly married printing press operator from Charlton, close to death. The end of George's war and possibly his life.

'When a quiet man is moved to passion, it seems the very earth will shake.'

Francine Mathews

George's Army Documents

Statement of service, listing his postings and confirmation of his discharge.

Descriptive report on enlistment, 'apparent' age twenty-two, however, he was born in September 1894 and enlisted in November 1915, so he would have been twenty. However, 'apparent' may mean the age he looked as we know he didn't have his birth certificate at that time. Note the description of the tattoo—'Union Jack, French flag, anchor in laurel wreath, Irish harp (figurehead)' and note 'scars on right forearm'.

Reference card, confirming pension entitlement.

Military history sheet, confirming him being a part of the British Expeditionary Force (BEF) and date and details of his wounds.

War medal index card.

Victory Medal (example) awarded for service in an active theatre of war to those who received the War Medal.

British war medal (example) awarded to those who served in the Imperial forces during WWI.

Silver War badge, awarded to those who were discharged during military service so that they could be identified as being unable to serve due to their wounds.

To my knowledge, neither the medals or the silver war badge were ever worn, or shown to his grandchildren and they are nowhere to be found.

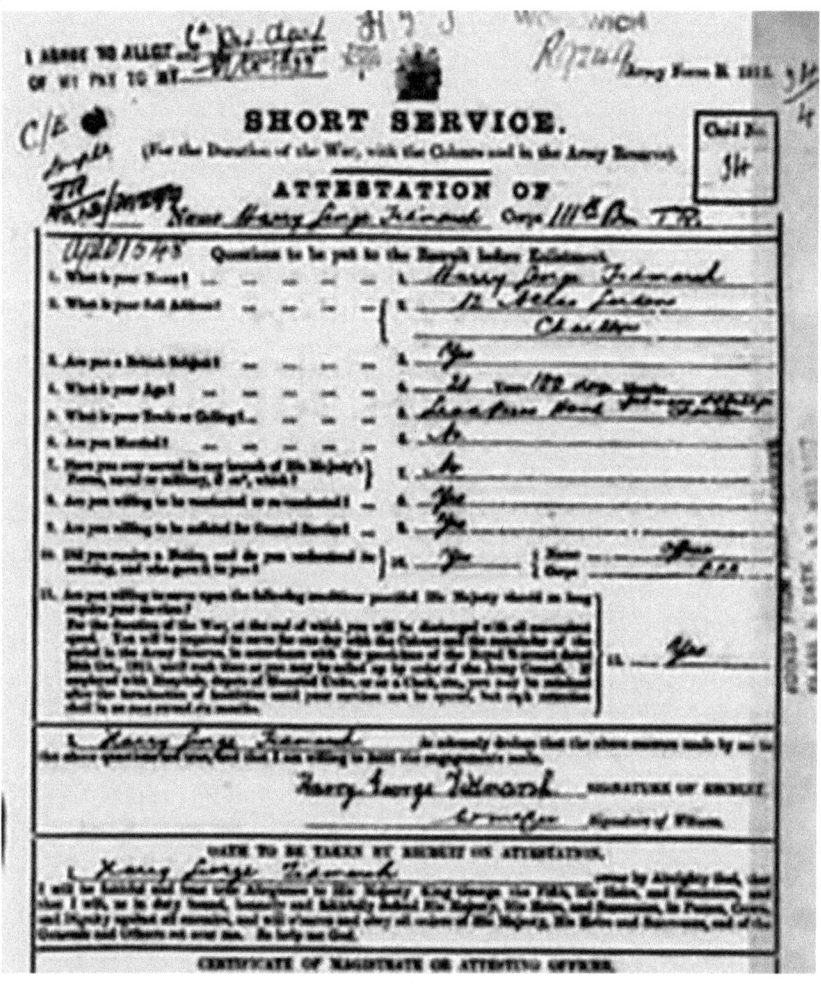

Short Service Attestation, a little blurred but basically a contract of allegiance between the volunteer and the army. Introduced by Kitchener in 1914 it's an agreement for George to serve three years or the duration of the war, whichever was longest, and not the normal enlistment period of twelve years. Although enlisting with the King's Royal Rifles, his attestation grouped him into the 111th Battalion Training Regiment. The small note in the top left-hand corner is George's instruction to pay 6d per day from his pay to his mother.

Certificate of discharge, 'not fit for war service', note the mention of his tattoo and wounds on bottom righthand corner.

Certificate of conduct whilst in military service—'has been good and proper'.

Epilogue

The Tomb of the Unknown Warrior

On 7 September 1920, in strictest secrecy, four unidentified British bodies were exhumed from temporary battlefield cemeteries in Ypres, Arras, the Asine and the Somme, four of the most terrible battlefields. None of the soldiers that did the digging were told why. The bodies were taken to GHQ, draped in a union flag and one body was chosen at random. A French honour guard stood over the coffin overnight. The following day, the selected body was placed inside a coffin made from oak from the grounds of Hampton Court. On top was placed a crusader's sword and a shield upon which was inscribed 'A British Warrior who fell in the Great War 1914–1918 for King and Country'. The following day, the coffin was loaded onto *HMS Vernon* and taken to Dover, where on arrival it was greeted with a nineteen-gun salute, a salute normally used only for field marshals, then by special train to Victoria Station. There it stayed overnight and on the morning of 11 November, was placed in a tomb in Westminster Abbey. His grave was filled using 100 sandbags of earth from the battlefields. When the Duke of York (soon to become George VI) married Elizabeth Bowes-Lyons in the abbey she left her wedding bouquet on the grave as a mark of respect (she had lost a brother in the war). Since then, all royal brides have sent back their wedding bouquets to be laid at the grave.

The intention was that all relatives of the 517,773 combatants whose bodies had not been identified could believe that the unknown warrior could well be their lost husband, father, brother or son.

The union flag draped over the coffin was an alter cloth used at the front.

The Hospitals

1918, the War is over, George returns to England, starts a new job and starts a family

It's possible that George may have started work at Lewisham Hospital, before moving on to the smaller Miller Hospital in Greenwich. He may even have worked briefly at Greenwich District Hospital as the Miller Hospital was being absorbed. A strange chapter to put in a family memoir you may think, but these places have featured in my family history since George started to work there after his discharge from the army in 1918 and he was immensely proud of his work, for reasons that will become apparent.

Lewisham Hospital

Built on the site of a workhouse bequeathed to the poor of the parish in 1612, which soon became overcrowded and was replaced with a newer building in 1817 'a three storied brick building in three blocks situated in the picturesque village of Lewisham'. Before long, it was already being used as a hospital until WWI when most of the workhouse residents were relocated and it became 'Lewisham Military Hospital'. The workhouse continued to function until 1929.

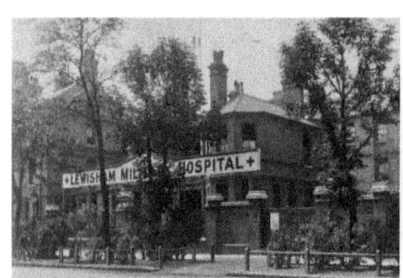

Courtesy of Lewisham and Greenwhich NHS Trust.

The Miller General Hospital

I'd never heard of the Miller. I always assumed the work-related stories I'd heard from Grandad were about the larger Lewisham Hospital, but when talking to my father, he mentioned the Miller and how he used to visit his dad and help him with the filing and the tidying up of the spiral bound notebooks that he and his team used to use. George was in charge of patient records by that time, so it seems his porter days were rewarded with a desk-based clerical job.

Whereas Lewisham Hospital was built on the site of a workhouse bequeathed to the poor of the parish, which soon grew into the monster that now exists, the Miller had a far more unique history.

I first had to scour the internet to find the place and came across a fascinating little website called 'Lost Hospitals of London'. The hospital's origins were in the Kent Dispensary, a small building opened in 1783 in Deptford. After Queen Victoria agreed to be its patron in 1837, its name changed to the Royal Kent Dispensary and its subsequent growth forced it to move to a brand-new building in Greenwich High Road in 1855. In 1883 it was decided to build a hospital in the grounds of the dispensary. The Miller General Hospital opened in 1884, with twenty-five beds, although this grew quickly. Interestingly, it was the first hospital to have circular wards, the theory being that corners harboured germs. Like Lewisham, part of the hospital was converted for wounded men from the Western Front. By WWII ten out of its 170 beds were set aside for military wounded. In 1948 it joined the NHS and by 1965 it had been absorbed into Greenwich District Hospital as the Miller General Wing, a few years after George retired. The sad end to the Miller came in 1975 when it was demolished. The original dispensary survived and has been converted into an apartment block.

The original dispensary building, all that's left of what used to the be the Miller General Hospital.

According to the 1911 census, George's occupation whilst living in West Ham was a dock labourer. After the move to Charlton, his occupation is 'lead pressman' which originally, I took to be some sort of engineering job, but it may well have been as a print press operator. However, due to his injuries affecting both his leg and arm, this was work he was no longer able to do. It may well be that he found work through the War Office route but regardless, he managed to find a job that he seemed to enjoy very much.

On reflection, things could have been worse, nearly 6 million British and German men were disabled by injury or disease, as many as 41,000 limbless men returned to Britain from the war. According to the National Archives, workshops were set up in local hospitals by the Ministry of Labour for ex-soldiers to learn new trades whilst waiting for treatment. The work carried out in setting up the workshops and the studies made of the men handling tools with their disabilities was the foundation for the advancement in the invention of better aids for disabled people and the understanding of their particular needs.

The life of a porter was somewhat different in the early twentieth century in that George's likeability and intelligence meant that he very often helped surgeons out with their operations if they were short-handed in theatre. I can remember him reeling off names of surgeons and doctors who relied on him to assist when needed. He also seemed to have an encyclopaedic knowledge of the human body and the process of many operations, but then his audience was young, eager and in awe and he was a Tidmarsh after all, so he already knew everything! As a reality check, my father remembers him regularly reading a medial encyclopaedia, hence his subject matter knowledge and him regaling his sons with how famous surgeons would 'call for George' and of course, ask for his advice. My cousin recalls: 'Our dad always used to diagnose illnesses and when Mum asked him if he was now a doctor, he used to reply that consultants consulted Grandad and he learned all he knew from him!'

Some photos featuring George as part of a visual training guide for the administering of what I would think is insulin. I contacted Lewisham Hospital to see if they had any records of this, but due to refurbishment, their records are stored offsite for the next two years. I am sending these photos to them for their archives at their request.

Family and Reflections

A relationship spanning decades

Portrait (my personal favourite).

Wedding photo.

Family event.

Three generations of the Tidmarsh family

There are another two generations to add, at the time of writing.

George, Some Reflections from His Grandchildren
A Falling Out

George told a story of an event upon the death of his mother. When he reached the family home to read his parents will, he arrived to find all of the furniture removed. Given that the only people other than him capable of this were Tilley or Frederick, it narrows the field a bit. Grandad didn't speak to either of them from that moment onwards and along with his reticence to share his war experiences, it made it very difficult for my aunty to get much information out of him when she was researching the family history. He never really wanted to open up about family, his father or his wartime experiences. Much like his tattoo, it was nothing to concern anyone else. My father, when attending Woolwich college, was in the same class as a girl with the same surname, when he enquired about her name, it transpired that she was his cousin, Jean, daughter of his uncle Frederick, one of many relatives he was unaware of because of the falling out.

Aunt Doll

The problem I referred to earlier, after the death of Florence, was what to do with Edith Alice, or Aunt Doll as she was affectionately known to us. Doll (I never knew her as anything else) was mentally incapable of work and was referred to as mentally ill in censuses since childhood. There is a story that Dolls mother contracted syphilis from her husband whilst she was pregnant, which resulted in her mental illness. I don't have evidence of this, but the fact was, she was incapable of looking after herself. By this time George and Daisy had moved to one King Alfred Avenue, a large double-fronted council house in Bellingham, overlooking a small green, protected from the outside world by a privet hedge, trimmed with military precision. On the event of the death of Florence, none of George's brothers or sisters offered to help with her, which left

George who out of duty and in accordance with his moral code offered to take her in. It took some persuading, but George eventually convinced Daisy that Doll should live with them. She stayed with George and Daisy until her death and had her own room downstairs, opposite one of the sitting rooms. She lived a quiet, I think happy, life until her death in 1964. My cousins and I have many memories of Doll. There were mixed opinions. Some found her a little scary, some found her friendly, some remember her opening the biscuit tin for them when Daisy wasn't looking. Some remember scars or marks, but others don't, she had a 'chubby, long face and shoulder length grey hair parted in the middle'. Some of my cousins were bathed by her and always remember how pleased she was to see them, as do I. None of us recall her ever saying much, if anything, as she couldn't talk properly so just mumbled. For me, she was always a quiet, gentle woman who, when we visited as children, made the tea, served on a tray in the living room, a slight, greying, quiet woman with a lovely smile, who loved children and was always to be seen wearing tartan slippers with bobbles on.

My cousins Sue and Kay have clearer recollections as they were around when Doll was younger and a little more active. 'It was Doll's job to do the washing and drying up, but I remember Nan would always carry the china herself to the cupboard at the back of the sitting room.'

The Tidmarsh–Notman Wedding and the Missing Hat

Even though George returned from the war a quieter, more introspective person, there were still times when this view could be challenged. The 17 July 1948 sees the wedding of Frederick Tidmarsh, eldest son of George and Daisy, and Ida Notman. My cousin recalls: '(Our aunty) Barbara was a bridesmaid, Mum made Barbara's dress. Dad told me there was a big furore at the party. My other grandad was a snob, though Nanna wasn't. A waiter gave

Nanny a glass of sherry. She said she didn't want it but would like a whisky. The waiter replied that he would have to ask Mr Notman to which Nan replied that, as she had bought the whisky for the event, she was having one.' There followed an altercation about a top hat and the inference from Mr Notman that George didn't have one, followed by George instructing the Tidmarshes present that they were leaving—which they did!

Advice

Before Daisy's daughter Barbara and her husband Ron moved into their own home. They lived with George and Daisy; downstairs it was possible to have separate space. Two of my cousins, Sandra and Steven, were raised there, leaving in 1965, a year after the death of Doll (Sandra still has her white sticks). This memory from Sandra is a very poignant recollection for me.

'I noted you're focusing on Grandad, who is the only man I have truly loved. There has never been such a wonderful man to have ever lived. He always gave me advice, which was wholly nuturing and true throughout my teenage years. I still remember things when we lived with them and Aunt Doll (I have her white walking canes tucked away somewhere). I still believe Grandad is my guide and inspiration, never will there be another man to match the love I feel for him.'

The Blue Bird

When I was very young, the age escapes me, I went to our local church Christmas bazaar. It was customary for us to buy a little something for our grandparents and I decided on the purchase of a blue china bird. It cost pennies, but I thought it was nice, so bought it. Daisy had a large hardwood dresser at the back of their living room, upon which she had wedding photos of all of her children plus a few souvenirs. One of the things she had on display was a small brass bell lady, very popular in the 50s and 60s, which my cousin now has. When she received the blue bird she seemed to take a liking to it, so she put it on her dresser and there it stayed. When she moved into the care home, her house was cleared and my Mum took the blue bird and gave it back to me. I still have it.

Canaries

When entering one King Alfred Ave, usually the first thing you heard was the sound of the two canaries they had in cages against wall at the front of the house. Sometimes the singing became so loud that Daisy put covers over them, fooling them into thinking it was night time—neat trick. When they went into a home, I took them and looked after them until they died of old age. Every time they sang, which was a lot, it took me back to my grandparents house.

Angel Fish

I went to a hospital once with Mum when I was a very young child, I will assume it was the Miller. She was visiting a friend I think and Grandad came and looked after me in the main reception. I remember a large (it seemed large to me at the time) aquarium, within which were large yellow and black striped Angel fish. Noticing my wonderment at these fish (which still remains to this day), George then proceeded to tell me that they had been trodden on—hence why they were flat and hence why they were in hospital. Upon relaying this fascinating fact to Mum, I was not a little shocked to find that my grandad had not been entirely honest, much to my embarrassment and Mum's amusement.

Punishment

My brother has a nice story about the punishment carried out by George, at Daisy's instruction, which involved him taking the offending boys upstairs to be hit with his walking stick. George, with the compassion borne of his experiences I think, hit his stick on the bed instead of his boys and told them to shout out at the right time.

Call for George!

As a porter, he enjoyed mixing with the doctors and consultants, quickly earning their respect and actually helping out in surgical wards when they were understaffed. He particularly enjoyed assisting with post-mortems and my brother recalls he was told by George that he enjoyed weighing brain mass. He knew all of the surgeons and consultants and could recite in detail many surgical operations.

Australia

Australia in the 1950s was young and exciting and desperately seeking skilled immigrants from the old world. The Empire was over, the new days of Commnwealth had begun and many British families answered the call to start a new life. One of those was George's second son, my uncle Harry, who arrived in Adelaide in 1950 on the P&O steamship *SS Malloja*. Things were very different then, my cousin Kay remembers: 'We have the shipping reccords from Port Adelaide where they arrived, in January 1950, in the blazing heat and we had to stay in army barracks for six months. This year, this part of the Tidmarsh family have been in Australia for seventy-three years.'

The reason I mention this is that a trip was organised for George and Daisy to visit the Aussie Tidmarshes. At this time, international passenger transport was in its infancy and their mode of transport was a commercial steamship with a total of twenty-four passengers and an Asian crew, none of whom spoke English. The journey took two months and had to anchor offshore when arriving at ports along the way as there were explosives as part of the cargo. They dined at the captain's table every night but suffered from boredom as you would expect. I remember Grandad telling me a story about how he was standing on deck when a shoal of flying fish flew over the ship—a fish story more beleivable than the Angel fish one. I'm not entirely sure what George thought about Australia, as he had mixed opinions, but what an adventure.

Here are some recollections from my cousins:

Roger: 'My memory is that they took nearly two months to get to Adelaide on a commercial ship with only twenty-four passengers and it had to anchor offshore as it was carrying munitions. I was still at school and when they arrived it was test match time. Having never grown up with any relatives it was a whole new experience. I went to the butcher's with grandma once. She told him off for wrapping the meat before she had inspected it. Before that, as a kid, I remember they sent me a "Boy's Own" annual book that was brilliant and had a pound note in it, which related to two pounds and five shillings in Aussie pounds, a lot of money. Grandma was very active and I had to run to keep up with her, Grandad was not very mobile and sat down most of the time.

'The only time I ever saw them again was in the 80s and they were in a small room in I guess an old folks' home. Grandma was not really responsive and had no idea who I was, but Grandad was as sharp as a tack and actually remembered more about his time in Australia than I did. Blesssed to know them.'

Kay: 'I remember it was a tramp steamer and Nanny was worried about the poor Lascar (Asian/Indian) crew, who she thought got treated very badly. And yes, it took so long like Roger said and they got fed up with having nothing much to do. I loved the Christmas boxes and later found out that they ordered them from a shop that shipped them over. One for girls and one for boys. Loved the books and the girls' annual and makeup and things Mum would never buy me. I used to think Nanny chose them herself!'

All of his grandchildren have very fond memories and there are so many stories. Some are here, some will remain personal, some will be shared at a later date in some form or another I suspect.

But before him, there were generations of Tidmarshes with stories to tell that reflect the history of their time, which one can only guess at, and also the stories of those generations yet to come.

Nearing the end

The final days of George and Daisy were spent in a care home in Somertrees Avenue in Grove Park, Lewisham, from 1985. Needless to say, the compassion of the local authorities knew no bounds and their savings, such as they were, were taken to contribute towards the care home costs. The real world sometimes shows little respect for those that made it possible. My mother recalled the story of the visit to one King Alfred Avenue of a representative of the local authorities who asked them if they had any savings, if so, they would be forfeit towards their care. 'He could have told them anything but being such an honest man, he told the truth.'

He could have lied, but then that wouldn't be him.

Their room was small and they spent most of their time together, especially after Daisy suffered a stroke. There was no en-suite and my brother, who visited many times, recalls how George fell over once and as a result used a zimmer frame instead of his famous walking sticks.

My cousin recalls, 'I found Grandad's birth certificate and he was registered George Harry Tidmarsh, born 3 August 1894 (author's note: Remember the confusion about his actual name, which remained a bit of a mystery for decades). Curiously, the telegram they received from the late queen on their seventieth anniversary was addressed to Mr and Mrs Harry George Tidmarsh, as was their wedding certificate which was amended later to George Harry Tidmarsh. I remember their seventieth anniversary, as the residents of Somertrees where they lived were all waiting for the party to start as they weren't normally allowed alcohol, but as it was a special occasion, they were all allowed to inbibe.'

Daisy died on 3 October 1988, George died within six months on 10 April 19. They had been married for over seventy-one years.

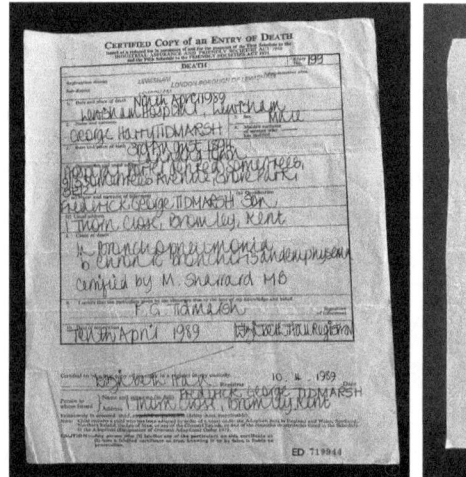

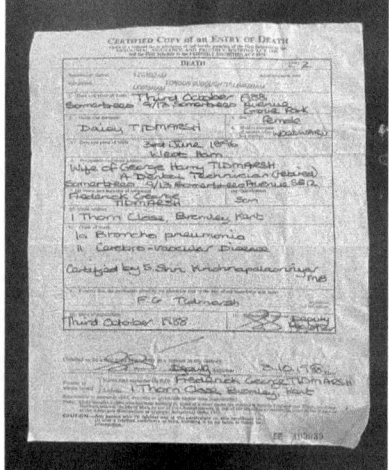

Certification of an end of an era.

The Water of Life

Kenneth William Tidmarsh

An indelible early memory of my father is his having a stiff left leg and never rolling up his long shirt sleeves, even on the hottest summer day. As children, my younger brother and I 'rode' his stiff leg in the childish hope that we might help to bend it. We never of course succeeded, but I remember him leaning back in his armchair as we rode, laughing aloud and putting in his own effort to enhance our ride. Looking back, I realise that it was probably very uncomfortable for him, knowing what I know now, but he was determined not to spoil our fun, as it were, and to cover his discomfort with laughter.

It is difficult for me to remember at what age I became aware of the fact that his disabilities were the result of his being wounded in the 'Great War' and also conscious of other men, comrades in arms and suffering, some blind with white sticks, some with an empty sleeve pinned across their jacket, some wheelchair bound. Despite his incapacity my father worked and was active with us children, playing cricket in our back garden and running his runs at a good limping pace. His 'speciality', however, was boxing. There were two pairs of boxing gloves in our house and as children we used to spar with him. We found it difficult to land a punch as he ducked, weaved and parried. Our only recourse was to bodily force him back against the wall on his stiff leg so that he lacked balance. His recourse then was to laughingly concede victory. I learned at a later age that he had been a talented amateur boxer and had got to his regimental final. Unfortunately, he lost. Had he won he would have been retained at the regimental base in England. He went to France.

I have further remembrances of my father which I thought were strange. In the summer on a hot day when we boys wore short sleeved shirts, my father in the garden would take off, or not wear a collar, but never roll up his sleeves. I only saw later in life why. He had deep 'trenches' on his left arm, shrapnel wounds, and on his right arm an elaborate tattoo with Britannia and Liberte bearing the union flag, a tattoo of which in later life he was embarrassed. As a grown-up, various facts of my father's condition were revealed to me. He dressed the wounds on his leg regularly and I realised later that he had had a running wound for over twenty years. I later learned that he had had numerous operations at the hospital where he worked as a porter, to remove splinters of shrapnel and bone. He kept a special set of forceps at home which in my later teens I would use to remove such splinters as they surfaced, without him having any sort of anaesthetic. It was only later, with the introduction of antibiotics that he was prescribed for a chest infection, that the wound was miraculously healed. My father never talked about the place or circumstance of his wounding until I was nearly forty years old, when he told me that he had been wounded at the dreadful Battle of Passchendaele. He had been hospitalised at Le Tréport in Belgium in a converted hotel where he was on the danger list for thirteen months and wanted to die. He had woken very early one summer morning feeling desperately thirsty. With no nurse on the ward to ask for a drink, he put his hand out the window by his bed to gather the morning dew to take from his fingers. The touch of the cool dew on his tongue brought my father to life. He decided he would live. The dew did not cure his wounds but it restored his spirit, which carried him through to his ninety-fifth year.

Happy Families

Reginald Stanley Tidmarsh

A Tidmarsh, George Harry, Dais' Woodward did marry
Though poor they were happy indeed
Of this wonderful pairing both loving and caring
Five children—the resultant seed

First there was Fred he's full of street 'cred'
And has been since he was a lad
He helped win the war and earned medals galore
But got only a couple—how sad

Second was Harry who's as happy as larry
With Christian beleifs like our mother
His views on creation engender elation
In many but not his young brother

THE TIDMARSH FAMILY TREE

The third, well that's Ken he's stacked full of 'gen'
His knowledge is boundless and rich
There's never a question nor yet a suggestion
He hasn't the answer to which

The fourth, Reg, a good bloke thinks life is a big joke
He never has been one for skiving
He's managed to keep his head just above water
By constantly ducking and diving

Barbara was rated though born quite belated
In the time scale that measures such things
Such joy and elation was bought to the nation
That the birth of a baby girl brings

Now we boys don't begrudge her becoming a judge
When she says speak plain, don't meander
If you won't give straight answers to questions she poses
Then duck or you'll get a right hander

After all that is said and all that is done
About altering one's life and the means
There's not much that can be accomplished by one
One's persona is all in the genes

One can't pick or choose them or make them nor lose them
They're inherited right from the start
Be happy enjoy them respect and employ them
And you will be happy at heart

Family Trees

Tidmarsh Family Tree from levels 1–12

Woodward Family Tree

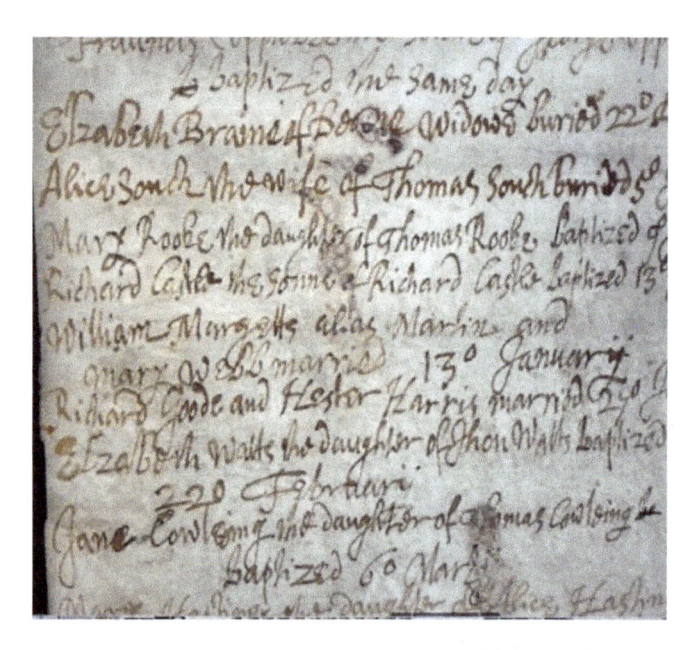

Tidmarsh Family Tree Data

Generation Level	Name	Relationship	Born	Died
1	John Tidmarsh	great x 10 grandfather	1570	1636
	Ann	wife of John	1570	1639
	Dinah Tidmarsh	daughter of John and Ann	unknown	unknown
2	Richard Tidmarsh	Son of John and Ann	1595	1663
	Mary Bartholomew	wife of Richard	1599	1634
	Mary Tidmarsh	daughter of Richard and Mary	unknown	1663
3	John Tidmarsh	**son of Richard and Mary**	1630	1728
	Mary Rooke	wife of John	1630	1686
4	John Tidmarsh	son of John and Mary	1666	1753
	Elizabeth Hiett	wife of John	1664	1730
5	Ann	daughter of John and Elizabeth	1688	1709
	Samuel	son of John and Elizabeth	1690	1771
	Elizabeth	daughter of John and Elizabeth	1696	unknown
	William Stayte	husband of Elizabeth	1688	unknown
	John	son of John and Elizabeth	1699	1777
	Thomas Tidmarsh	son of John and Mary	1686	1782
	Margaret Grimmett	wife of Thomas	1684	1764
6	Ann Tidmarsh	daughter of Thomas and Margaret	1711	unknown
	Elizabeth Tidmarsh	daughter of Thomas and Margaret	1712	unknown
	John Freeman	husband of Elizabeth		unknown
	John Tidmarsh	son of Thomas and Margaret	1714	unknown
	Samuel Tidmarsh	son of Thomas and Margaret	1716	unknown
	Thomas Tidmarsh	son of Thomas and Margaret	1719	unknown
	Frances Tidmarsh	daughter of Thomas and Margaret	1721	1726
	James Tidmarsh	son of Thomas and Margaret	1726	1727
	Edmund Tidmarsh	son of Thomas and Margaret	1730	unknown
	Richard Tidmarsh	son of Thomas and Margaret	1724	unknown
	Merrell Paxford	wife of Richard	1730	unknown

Level	Name	Relationship	Born	Died
7	Thomas	son of Richard and Merrell	1752	unknown
	Samuel (i)	son of Richard and Merrell	1754	1754
	John	son of Richard and Merrell	1755	unknown
	Ann	daughter of Richard and Merrell	1758	unknown
	Richard	son of Richard and Merrell	1760	unknown
	Elizabeth	daughter of Richard and Merrell	1762	unknown
	Sarah	daughter of Richard and Merrell	1764	unknown
	Margaret (i)	daughter of Richard and Merrell	1766	1771
	Samuel (ii)	son of Richard and Merrell	1768	unknown
	Margaret (ii)	daughter of Richard and Merrell	1770	unknown
	William	son of Richard and Merrell	1772	unknown
	Mary	daughter of Richard and Merrell	1778	unknown
	James Tidmarsh	son of Richard and Merrell	1773	1853
	Mary Edens	wife of Richard	1772	1856
8	John	son of James and Mary	1802	unknown
	Elizabeth Bartlett	1st wife of John	1807	1830
	Anne Smith	2nd wife of John	1812	1899
	Richard	son of James and Mary	1804	1804
	Anne	daughter of James and Mary	1805	1872
	Elihu Griffin	husband of Anne	1807	1880
	Elizabeth	daughter of James and Mary	1811	1849
	William Townsend	husband of Elizabeth	1816	unknown
	Jane	daughter of James and Mary	1814	1851
	Charles Paxford	husband of Jane	1815	1843
	Thomas Tidmarsh	son of James Mary	1799	1847
	Martha Brooks	wife of Thomas	1809	1892
	William Pantin	2nd husband of Martha	1806	1873

THE TIDMARSH FAMILY TREE

Level	Name	Relationship	Born	Died
9	Jane Tidmarsh	daughter of Thomas and Martha	1828	1917
	Eliiza	daughter of Jane	1850	unknown
	William Tidmarsh	son of Thomas and Martha	1830	1886
	Fanny Tidmarsh	daughter of Thomas and Martha	1832	1856
	James Tidmarsh	son of Thomas and Martha	1834	1896
	John Tidmarsh	son of Thomas and Martha	1844	1853
	Rueben Tidmarsh	son of Thomas and Martha	1845	1926
	Elizabeth Langford	wife of Reuben	1851	1925
	Mary Tidmarsh	daughter of Thomas	1839	1926
10	Ann Tidmarsh	daughter of Mary and Unknown	1854	1873
	Frederick Henry Stayte	husband of Mary	1841	1920
	George Stayte	son of Mary and Frederick	1868	1924
	Lizzie Selina Stayte	daughter of Mary and Frederick	1869	1921
	Lettie Stayte	daughter of Mary and Frederick	1870	1943
	Rosa Stayte	daughter of Mary and Frederick	1872	1959
	Thomas Tidmarsh	son of Mary and Unknown	1859	1926
	Sarah Flanagan	1st wife of Thomas	1862	1887
	Florence Tidmarsh	daughter of Thomas and Sarah	1883	1941
	Walter Sylvester Day	husband of Florence Tidmarsh	1883	1978
	Lily Maud Tidmarsh	daughter of Thomas and Sarah	1887	1887
11	Florence Day	daughter of Florence and Walter	1909	1993
	Charles Ranton	husband of Florence Day	1882	1972
	Florence Tidmarsh (nee Woodley)	2nd wife of Thomas	1869	1935
	George Harry	son of Thomas and Florence	1894	1989
	Daisy Woodwood	wife of George	1896	1988

Level	Name	Relationship	Born	Died
	Tilley Tidmarsh	daughter of Thomas and Florence	1889	unknown
	Edith Alice (Aunt Doll)	daughter of Thomas and Florence	1890	1964
	William Thomas	son of Thomas and Florence	1892	1923
	Nellis (Nellie) Tidmarsh	daughter of Thomas and Florence	1896	1974
	Will J Green	husband of Nellie	1896	1955
	Frederick Charles	son of Thomas and Florence	1903	1974
	Ellen Smith	wife of Frederick	1903	1984
	Cicilia Parkin	adopted daughter	1909	unknown
12	Frederick George	son of George and Daisy	1919	2010
	Ida Joan Notman	wife of Frederick	1924	2005
	Harry William Thomas	son of George and Daisy	1921	2010
	Patricia Mary Parlour	wife of Harry	1920	2014
	Kenneth William	son of George and Daisy	1928	2020
	Audrey Eileen Taylor	wife of Ken	1927	2010
	Reginald Stanley	son of George and Daisy	1930	
	Doreen Rose Howard	wife of Reginald	1932	
	Barbara May	daughter of George and Daisy	1937	2020
	Ronald Sydney Tame	husband of Barbara	1933	2010

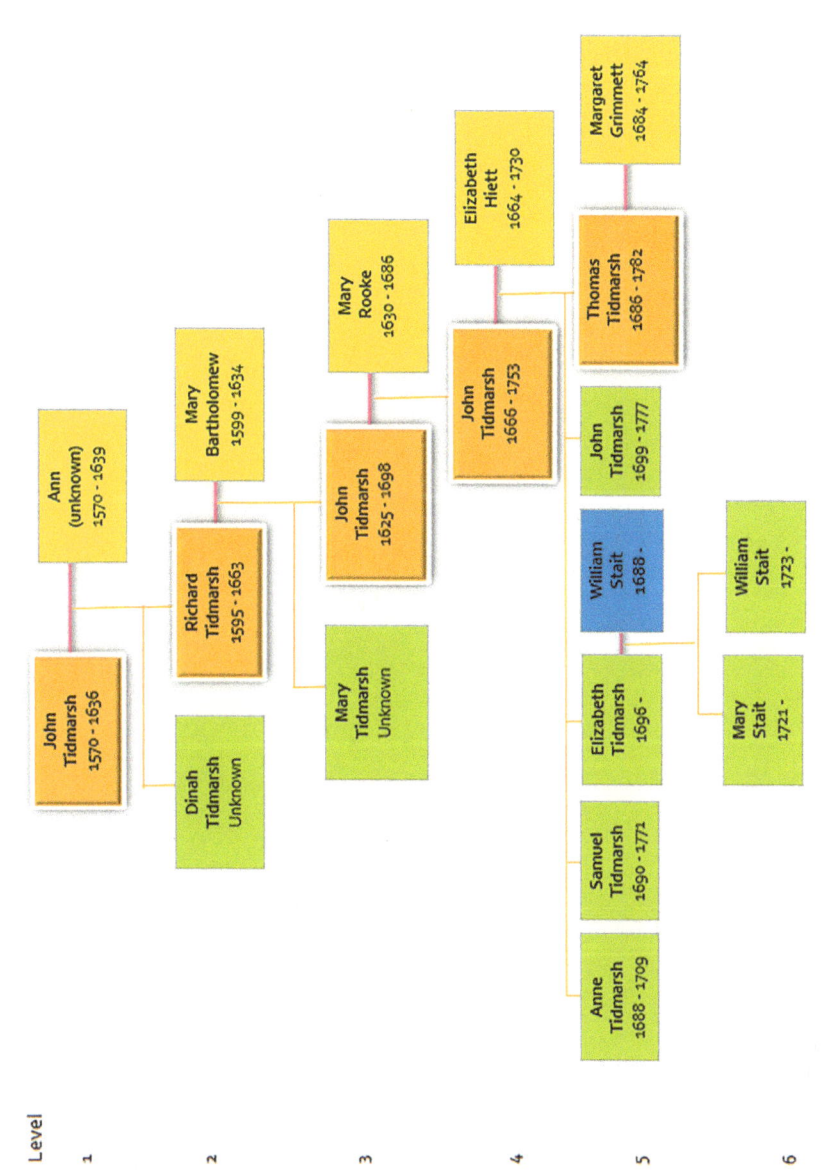

The Tidmarsh Tree Plan Part 1: Levels 1–5

Level

1

- John Tidmarsh 1570 - 1636
- Ann (unknown) 1570 - 1639

2

- Richard Tidmarsh 1595 - 1663
- Mary Bartholomew 1599 - 1634
- Dinah Tidmarsh Unknown

3

- John Tidmarsh 1625 - 1698
- Mary Rooke 1630 - 1686
- Mary Tidmarsh Unknown

4

- John Tidmarsh 1666 - 1753
- Elizabeth Hiett 1664 - 1730
- Thomas Tidmarsh 1686 - 1782
- Margaret Grimmett 1684 - 1764

5

- Anne Tidmarsh 1688 - 1709
- Samuel Tidmarsh 1690 - 1771
- Elizabeth Tidmarsh 1696 -
- William Stait 1688 -
- John Tidmarsh 1699 - 1777

6

- Mary Stait 1721 -
- William Stait 1723 -

The Tidmarsh Tree Plan Part 2: Levels 6-12

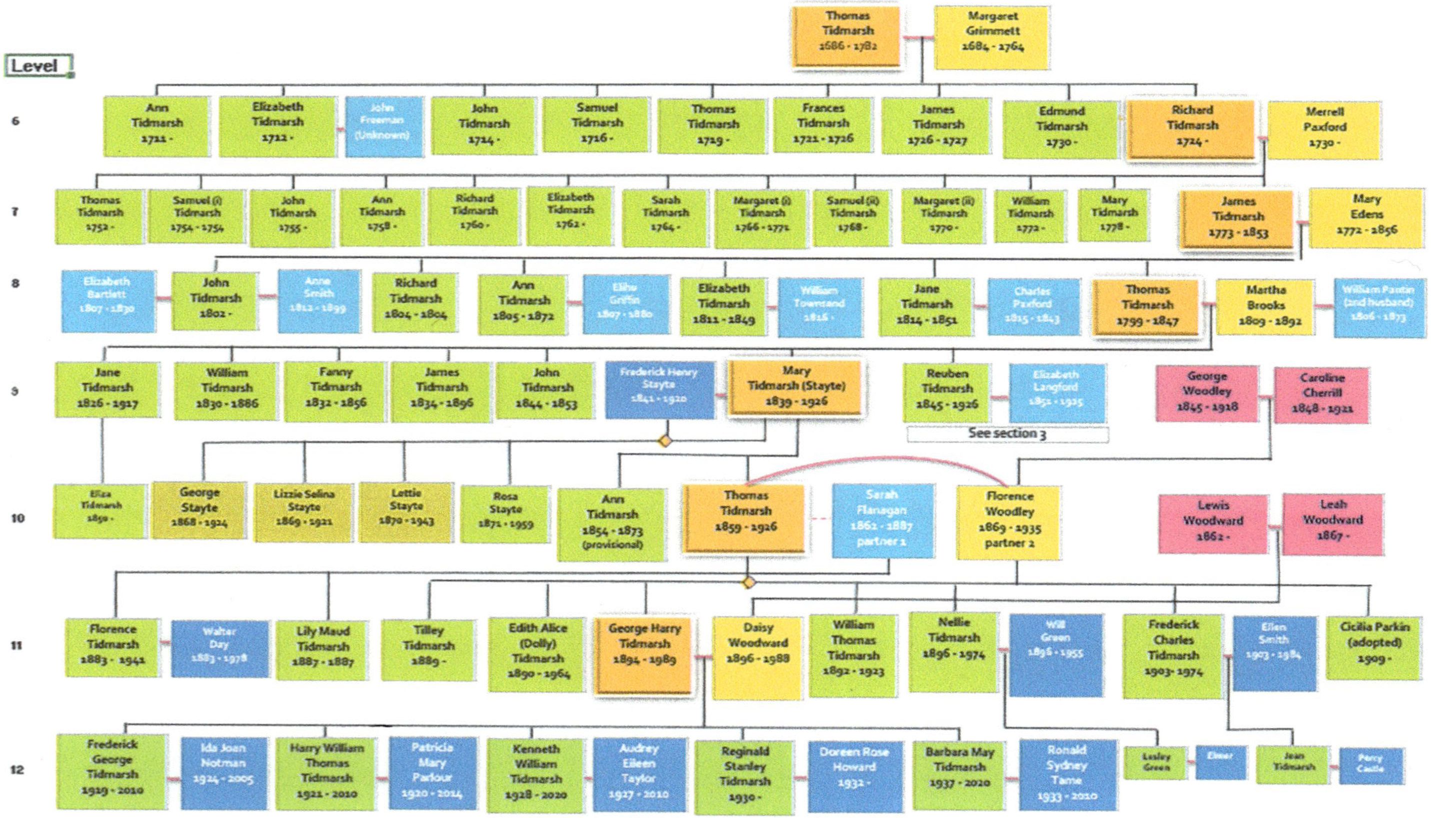

Level 6:
- Thomas Tidmarsh 1686-1782 — Margaret Gimmett 1684-1764
- Merrell Paxford 1739-
- Ann Tidmarsh 1721-
- Elizabeth Tidmarsh 1721-
- John Tidmarsh 1724-
- Samuel Tidmarsh 1716-
- Thomas Tidmarsh 1719-
- Frances Tidmarsh 1721-1726
- James Tidmarsh 1726-1727
- Edmund Tidmarsh 1730-
- Richard Tidmarsh 1724-

Level 7:
- Thomas Tidmarsh 1752-
- Samuel (i) Tidmarsh 1754-1754
- John Tidmarsh 1755-
- Ann Tidmarsh 1758-
- Elizabeth Tidmarsh 1762-
- Richard Tidmarsh 1760-
- Sarah Tidmarsh 1764-
- Samuel (ii) Tidmarsh 1768-
- Margaret (i) Tidmarsh 1766-1771
- Margaret (ii) Tidmarsh 1770-
- William Tidmarsh 1773-
- Mary Tidmarsh 1778-
- James Tidmarsh 1773-1853 — Mary Eden 1772-1856
- William Paxton (2nd husband) 1806-1873
- Martha Brooks 1809-1891

Level 8:
- John Freeman (Unknown)
- Elizabeth Bartlett 1807-1852
- Anne Smith 1812-1899
- Ellen Griffin 1807-1880
- William Townend 1816-
- Elizabeth Tidmarsh 1811-1849
- Jane Tidmarsh 1814-1851
- Charles Paxford 1815-1843
- Thomas Tidmarsh 1799-1847
- Caroline Cherrill 1843-1921
- Leah Woodward 1869-

Level 9:
- Jane Tidmarsh 1826-1917
- John Tidmarsh 1802-
- Richard Tidmarsh 1804-
- James Tidmarsh 1834-1896
- Ann Tidmarsh 1805-1872
- John Tidmarsh 1844-1853
- Frederick Stayte 1811-1910
- Reuben Tidmarsh 1845-1926
- Elizabeth Langford 1863-1935
- George Woodley 1845-1918

Level 10:
- Eliza Tidmarsh 1850-
- William Tidmarsh 1830-1886
- Fanny Tidmarsh 1832-1856
- Mary Tidmarsh (Stayte) 1839-1926
- Ann Tidmarsh 1854-1873 (protracted)
- Sarah Flanagan 1862-1887 partner 1
- Thomas Tidmarsh 1859-1926
- Florence Woodley 1869-1935 partner 2
- (See section 3)

Level 11:
- George Stayte 1868-1924
- Lizzie Selina Stayte 1869-1921
- Little Stayte 1870-1943
- Rosa Stayte 1871-1959
- Tilley Tidmarsh 1889-
- Edith Alice (Dolly) Tidmarsh 1890-1961
- Daisy Woodward 1896-1988
- William Thomas Tidmarsh 1892-1913
- Nellie Tidmarsh 1896-1974
- Will Green 1895-1955
- Frederick Charles Tidmarsh 1909-1974
- Ellen Smith 1903-1982
- Cecilia Parkin (adopted) 1909-

Level 12:
- Walter Day 1883-1918
- Lily Maud Tidmarsh 1887-1887
- Florence Tidmarsh 1883-1941
- Frederick George Tidmarsh 1919-2010
- Ida Joan Norman 1924-2005
- Harry William Thomas Tidmarsh 1921-2010
- Patricia Mary Parlour 1930-2014
- Kenneth William Tidmarsh 1928-2020
- Audrey Eileen Taylor 1927-2010
- Reginald Stanley Tidmarsh 1930-
- Doreen Rose Howard 1931-
- Barbara May Tidmarsh 1937-2020
- Ronald Sydney Tame 1933-2010
- Lesley Green
- Elinor
- Jean Tidmarsh
- Percy Cade

The Tidmarsh Tree Plan Part 3: Reuben and Elizabeth

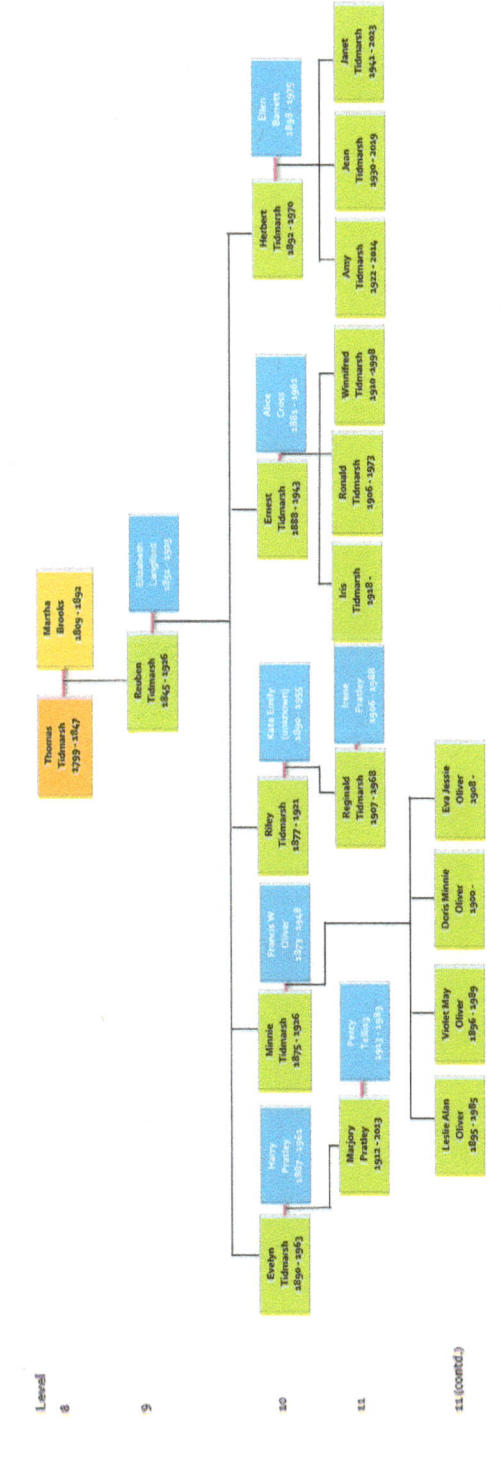

Level

8
- Thomas Tidmarsh 1799-1847
- Martha Brooks 1809-1852

9
- Reuben Tidmarsh 1845-1916
- Elizabeth Langford 1851-1915

10
- Evelyn Tidmarsh 1850-1963
- Harry Pratley 1877-1961
- Minnie Tidmarsh 1875-1906
- Francis W Oliver 1873-1948
- Riley Tidmarsh 1877-1921
- Kate Emily (unknown) 1859-1955
- Ernest Tidmarsh 1888-1943
- Alice Cross 1881-1961
- Herbert Tidmarsh 1893-1970
- Ellen Barrett 1898-1973

11
- Marjory Pratley 1912-2003
- Percy Tellog 1911-1989
- Leslie Alan Oliver 1895-1985
- Violet May Oliver 1896-1989
- Doris Minnie Oliver 1900-
- Eva Jessie Oliver 1908-
- Reginald Tidmarsh 1907-1968
- Irene Pratley 1906-1968
- Iris Tidmarsh 1918-
- Ronald Tidmarsh 1906-1973
- Winnifred Tidmarsh 1910-1998
- Amy Tidmarsh 1922-2014
- Jean Tidmarsh 1930-2009
- Janet Tidmarsh 1941-2003

11 (cont'd.)

The Woodward Family Tree

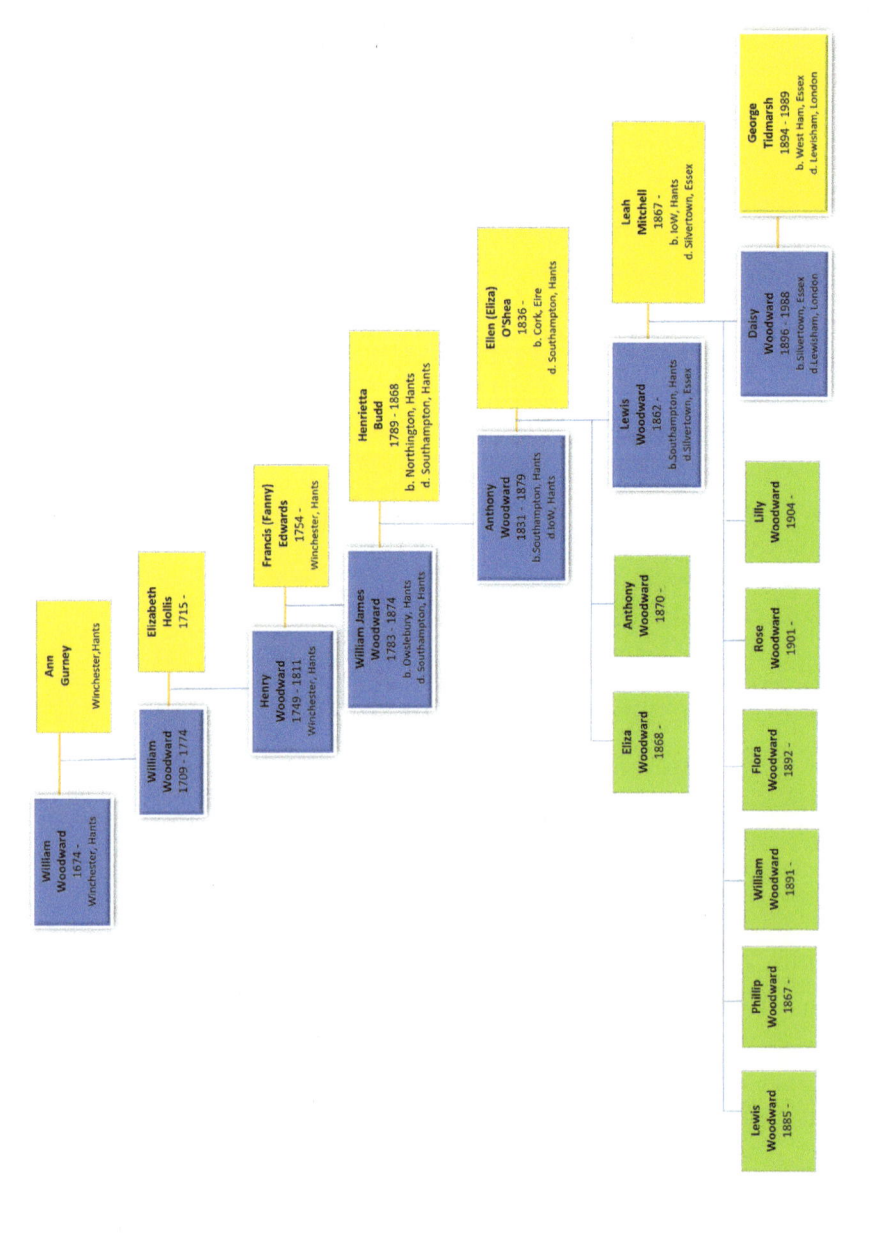

- **William Woodward** 1674 - , Winchester, Hants
  - m. **Ann Gurney**, Winchester, Hants
  - **William Woodward** 1709 - 1774
    - m. **Elizabeth Hollis** 1715 -
    - **Henry Woodward** 1749 - 1811, Winchester, Hants
      - m. **Francis (Fanny) Edwards** 1754 - , Winchester, Hants
      - **William James Woodward** 1783 - 1874, b. Owslebury, Hants, d. Southampton, Hants
        - m. **Henrietta Budd** 1789 - 1868, b. Northington, Hants, d. Southampton, Hants
        - **Anthony Woodward** 1831 - 1879, b. Southampton, Hants, d. IoW, Hants
          - m. **Ellen (Eliza) O'Shea** 1836 - , b. Cork, Eire, d. Southampton, Hants
          - **Lewis Woodward** 1862 - , b. Southampton, Hants, d. Silvertown, Essex
            - m. **Leah Mitchell** 1867 - , b. IoW, Hants, d. Silvertown, Essex
            - **Eliza Woodward** 1868 -
            - **Anthony Woodward** 1870 -
            - **Phillip Woodward** 1867 -
            - **Lewis Woodward** 1885 -
            - **William Woodward** 1891 -
            - **Flora Woodward** 1892 -
            - **Daisy Woodward** 1896 - 1988, b. Silvertown, Essex, d. Lewisham, London
              - m. **George Tidmarsh** 1894 - 1989, b. West Ham, Essex, d. Lewisham, London
            - **Rose Woodward** 1901 -
            - **Lilly Woodward** 1904 -

Conclusion

The continuation of a family line from an Anglo-Saxon homestead in Berkshire, to the Cotswolds, east London docklands, the bloody fields of northern France and the council estates of south-east London, the result of generations past and the legacy of generations to follow.

Appendix 1

Notes from Audrey's research, note the reference to contact with distant relatives in Stonesfield and their intention to visit.

> Re the Family Tree we have not tried to go back any further than James and Mary from Fawler. A very small village near Stonesfield - no church hence baptisms at Charlbury. Why was Mary the only one not baptised - maybe we shall never know.
>
> As you see she had two illegitimate children, in particular our Thomas. Our missing section is from then right up to Sarah Flanagan. She said she was married on Florence's cert. but we cannot find it.
>
> Thomas, when he married Florence Woodley gave his father's name as Thomas Tidmarsh. So far we have not found any evidence of Mary, his mother, marrying. The Registrar at West Ham reckons people gave their grandfathers name - in lieu of father, and Thomas Tidmarsh was his grandfather
>
> Regarding Reuben, the youngest brother of Mary. The only one apart from William, that we have any details of. There are gravestones in Stonesfield for him and wife and all his children. His youngest son Herbert married Ellen and they had a child Janet - who we are now in contact with and hope to go to Stonesfield soon to meet her. She is in contact with two elderly female cousins Winnie and Iris, surviving children of Ernest. She is going to try to find out if they have any remembrances.
>
> We still have so many queries and gaps. How weird that Thomas and more particularly his wife Florence, took on the young Florence from his former liaison. So far we have not found that Sarah Flanagan died young. We still hope for a breakthrough in finding the grandfather and grandmother that Ken's father talked a lot about. Was it Mary? But she married and therefore was not a Tidmarsh. We have even wondered whether it was Florence Woodley's parents but Ken does not think so for various reasons.

Appendix 2

An email from Neil Melrose of Stonesfield village:

On 4 October 2023, I received an email from Neil Melrose. Neil lives at Wisteria Cottage in Stonesfield and in talking to the churchwarden, Lindsey Sellar, she told him that she had helped Karen and me with our family tree. Unknown to Lindsey was that Neil's wife was a Tidmarsh. Upon talking to Neil, I found that his wife, Janet, was the granddaughter of Reuben and Elizabeth Tidmarsh, her father being Herbert Tidmarsh. Unfortunately, Janet passed away on 22 July 2023 at the age of eighty-two. They had been married for fifty-seven and a half years.

Audrey mentions two elderly cousins, Iris and Winnie, who were children of Reuben and Elizabeth's son, Ernest, that she hoped one day to meet.

Neil and Janet were in constant touch with Sue O'Brien, who is the adopted daughter of Percy and Marjorie Telling (see level 11 of the Reuben and Elizabeth tree). Percy and Marjorie lost their only son, Dennis, many years ago. Janet's mother was a Barrett and there are still Barretts in and around Stonesfield and surrounding villages.

Neil has a good friend, Michael Green. Michael is a local farmer and owns 'Green Farms' (www.greenfarms.co.uk). Michael is a keen local historian and has carried out extensive research on several local families in Oxfordshire, one of which is the Tidmarshes. I am in receipt of his work, which I have not included in this story but hopefully will include in the next one. I couldn't contact Michael at the time as he was harvesting his potato crop! I'm thinking now that, centuries ago, many of our ancestors would have been involved in harvesting, working for people like Michael.

Appendix 3

A letter from Reg to his brother Ken and Audrey upon first reading their family tree.

41 Haven Close
Swanley, Kent
BR8 7JY
28 February 07

Ken/Audrey, Hi!

Thank you Audrey for the family tree, your very clear explanations and to you both for your investigations. I believe you mentioned, some way back, that there appeared to be a/some skeleton/s in the family cupboard and I think that I see what you mean, even though genealogy be not one of my better subjects!

I am typing this on my computer so that I can file same for some future enquiries that I may make. Should I be able to throw any light on certain 'dark' entries, this will require a specific meet.

I will be preparing a chart and of course you will be the first recipients. Meanwhile, I return your diagram and letter, which I have copied, so that we will all be 'singing from the same hymn sheet'.

NOW, as I see it, as true genealogy goes, our surname should not be Tidmarsh, UNLESS – horror of horrors – this (the unthinkable) is the first skeleton!! My suspicions arise from Mary b. 1839 being the only one of the seven children not to be baptised (parents choice soon after birth). Mary had her children, Thomas and Ann, baptised and Ann confirmed, eleven years later! Do you think Thomas and Ann could have been twins?

I mentioned what sparked my interest, being Michael's, uncanny, mutual friendship with a guy he meets at the 'pub' when they watch top flight soccer games. It was only after some time that they exchanged surnames. M's friend says he remembers an aunt Ellen Tidmarsh. Could this not be Herbert (out of Reuben Tidmarsh) his wife Ellen (nee A Name.) Tidmarsh?

With regard to the old Tidmarsh photographs, we certainly never had any, other than a copy of Mum's parents and one of a very young (engagement?) Mum & Dad. Surely Fred or Barbara would be the most likely to have these?

Robert is family orientated and he has a copy of Dad in his army uniform, which he either got from Barbara or Fred's, Susan. Must make a few enquiries.

Luv,

Reg

Afterword

It is my hope that this story will inspire an additional volume, not only to scoop up things I have overlooked or to include information that I have been unable to find, but to continue the family tree from level 12 onwards to my cousins and me and our children and our children's children.

There are still many stories to be told and many characters to be included as it progresses. It's important, in my opinion, to understand your place in history, albeit seemingly insignificant, and take an interest in your family's place in it—it may help you to understand who you are and how you arrived at where you are now. It did for me, anyway.

'The loved are never forgotten.'

Milton Keynes UK
Ingram Content Group UK Ltd.
UKHW052344150224
437782UK00002B/31